Empowering Parents, Empowering Kids

Navigating the World of Strong-Willed Children A Comprehensive Parent's Handbook for Strong-Willed Solutions

TOSCA A. HAAG

Copyright © 2023 by TOSCA A. HAAG

All rights reserved. No part of this publication may be reproduced, distributed, or transmitted in any form or by any means, including photocopying, recording, or other electronic or mechanical methods, without the prior written permission of the publisher, except in the case of brief quotations embodied in critical reviews and certain other noncommercial uses permitted by copyright law.

ISBN: 978-1-83556-070-9 PAPERBACK

ISBN: 978-1-83556-071-6 HARDBACK

ISBN: 978-1-83556-072-3 EBOOK

Book Design by HMDPUBLISHING

Dedication

To my four beautiful, strong-willed (hard-headed) and brilliant children, Raven, Lynn, Crystal, and Brenton, who challenged me constantly. In the absence of internet resources or parenting magazines to guide me, I must have done something right.

With all my love,

Mom

Contents

INTRODUCTION 5

CHAPTER 1.
SET CLEAR BOUNDARIES 10

CHAPTER 2.
CONSISTENCY IS KEY 16

CHAPTER 3.
HOW TO OFFER CHOICES 22

CHAPTER 4.
EMPATHETIC LISTENING 33

CHAPTER 5.
ENCOURAGE INDEPENDENCE 38

CHAPTER 6.
NEGOTIATE 64

CHAPTER 7.
TESTING LIMITS 70

CHAPTER 8.
POSITIVE REINFORCEMENT 78

CHAPTER 9.
MODEL BEHAVIOR 83

CHAPTER 10.
PROBLEM- SOLVING SKILLS 92

CHAPTER 11.
AVOID POWER STRUGGLES 105

CHAPTER 12.
TEACH EMOTION REGULATION 118

CHAPTER 13.
TIME-OUTS 138

CHAPTER 14.
CONSISTENT CONSEQUENCES 145

CHAPTER 15.
QUALITY TIME 152

CHAPTER 16.
SEEK PROFESSIONAL HELP 159

INTRODUCTION

Strong-willed children possess a unique and formidable spirit that, while challenging for parents, can ultimately foster remarkable growth and development. These children exhibit an unwavering determination and independence from an early age, often displaying an unyielding stance about their preferences, desires, and beliefs. While parenting such individuals can be a daunting task, it is undeniably crucial for parents to take a major role in guiding them through life's challenges, as this can significantly affect their journey toward becoming strong and significant adults.

Strong-willed children, often described as having a strong or determined temperament, exhibit distinct characteristics that set them apart from what might be considered an "average" child. These characteristics don't have negative connotations, they just show a particular personality type. Here are some key differences:

People recognize strong-willed children for their persistence and determination as they relentlessly pursue what they want. They stick to their goals and can be relentless in pursuing what they want, even when faced with obstacles. This determination can be a valuable trait in adulthood, as it often leads to achieving ambitious goals.

Independent: Strong-willed children typically want more independence and autonomy than their peers. These children may exhibit self-reliance and a desire for autonomy more than their peers, showing strong potential for future leadership roles.

Questioning Authority: These children may question rules and authority figures more frequently than others. They have a strong need to understand the reasoning behind rules and may challenge them if they find them random or inconsistent.

High Energy and Enthusiasm: Strong-willed children have a surplus of energy and enthusiasm. This surplus of energy can often be called ADD by some people, so it is important to recognize the difference between that high level of natural energy and the "bouncing off the walls" energy caused by a diet of stimulating foods and high amounts of sugar. Strong-willed children can be highly enthusiastic and become engaged in activities they are passionate about and are often willing to put in extra effort to excel in their interests. This is an example of natural energy, not energy that comes from an overconsumption of sugary and stimulating foods.

Resilience: Strong-willed children are resilient in the face of setbacks and failures. They bounce back quickly from disappointments and view challenges as opportunities for growth.

Sound Sense of Self: These children often have a well-defined sense of self from an early age. They know their preferences and dislikes, and they do not succumb to peer pressure easily.

It's important to remember that strong-willed children are not inherently "difficult" or "troublesome." Instead, they have unique qualities that, when nurtured and channeled effectively, can lead to positive outcomes in adulthood. Parenting and teaching strong-willed children may require a more tailored approach that recognizes and encourages their strengths while providing clear boundaries and guidance to help them channel their determination and assertiveness in constructive ways.

One of the key aspects of nurturing strong-willed children is to recognize the potential within their spirited nature. Rather than attempting to suppress their innate tendencies, parents can help channel their energy in positive directions. By providing a supportive environment that encourages critical thinking, problem-solving, and self-expression, parents can mold these children into assertive and capable individuals who can stand up for themselves and their beliefs constructively.

Parents play a pivotal role in helping strong-willed children develop essential life skills, such as empathy, effective communication, and conflict resolution. These skills are crucial for building healthy relationships and navigating the complexities of the adult world. By engaging in open conversations, actively listening to their concerns, and teaching them how to consider different perspectives, parents can equip their children with the tools they need to interact successfully with peers, colleagues, and authority figures.

Guiding strong-willed children also involves setting clear boundaries and expectations. This provides them with a sense of structure and discipline while allowing room for their independent nature to flourish. When parents establish consistent rules and consequences, it helps these children understand the importance of accountability and responsible decision-making. This guidance lays the foundation for them to become adults who can navigate ethical dilemmas and societal norms with confidence.

Parents significantly influence the self-esteem and self-worth of strong-willed children. This cannot be overstated. By providing unconditional love and acceptance, parents bolster their children's self-confidence, assisting them to embrace their uniqueness without fear of rejection. When parents acknowledge their achievements, no matter how small, and offer constructive feedback during setbacks, they instill a resilient mindset that is crucial for handling life's challenges with grace and determination.

Providing unconditional love and acceptance to strong-willed children is essential for their healthy development. Unconditional love involves showing care, empathy, and support for a child regardless of their behavior or choices. This form of love communicates that their worth is not contingent on meeting certain conditions or expectations. By offering such love, parents create a secure emotional foundation that allows children to explore their independence and make mistakes without fearing rejection. This helps them to develop a strong sense of self and the confidence to face challenges head-on, knowing they are loved regardless of the outcomes.

Enabling involves inadvertently allowing or even encouraging negative behaviors or attitudes. While unconditional love respects a child's autonomy while maintaining healthy boundaries, enabling often involves bending or removing boundaries altogether to avoid conflict or discomfort. Enabling can prevent strong-willed children from learning crucial life lessons, consequences, and responsibilities. It shields them from the natural outcomes of their actions, preventing them from developing vital skills such as decision-making, problem-solving, and accountability. While unconditional love empowers children to embrace their authenticity and navigate life's difficulties, enabling may inadvertently hinder their personal growth and lead to potential challenges in adulthood.

Enabling a child's undesirable behaviors or shielding them from facing the consequences of their actions can hinder their overall development. When parents or caregivers constantly intervene to eliminate obstacles or difficulties, children miss out on valuable opportunities to learn problem-solving skills, emotional resilience, and accountability. This form of overprotection can create a dependency mindset, where children struggle to take initiative or hesitate making decisions independently, leading to a lack of self-confidence and an underdeveloped sense of responsibility. In the long run, enabling can impede a child's ability to cope with challenges, make sound judgments, and develop into a well-adjusted and capable adult.

The journey of strong-willed children toward becoming significant adults is a partnership between their inherent nature and the guidance provided by their parents. With the right approach, parents can harness the power of their child's determination, shaping it into a force that drives personal growth, resilience, and positive contributions to society. By embracing their role as mentors, supporters, and advocates, parents pave the way for these spirited individuals to emerge as strong, influential adults capable of making meaningful contributions to the world.

Dealing with strong-willed children can be both challenging and rewarding. Strong-willed children are often determined, independent, and opinionated, which are qualities that can serve them well in the long run. Remember, strong-willed children are often learning to assert themselves and develop important life skills. Your role as a parent or caregiver is to guide them while respecting their individuality and helping them learn how to navigate the world around them.

This book specifically offers strategies to assist parents in navigating and guiding their strong-willed child's behavior when simply removing their iPad is ineffective. This book should offer a better understanding of the nuts and bolts of handling strong-willed children and some examples of how to implement strategies for maximum effectiveness. I don't like books that give you a list of things to do, but don't tell you how to do them.

CHAPTER 1

SET CLEAR BOUNDARIES

As parents set boundaries during the formative years, they equip their children with valuable life skills that extend far beyond childhood. When kids learn to respect boundaries, they also learn about respecting others' space, opinions, and autonomy. This early exposure to limits fosters open communication between parents and children, as well as nurturing a sense of trust and understanding. Setting boundaries empowers children to navigate the complexities of the world, enabling them to make informed decisions and manage impulses. By initiating this process from a young age, parents lay the foundation for a healthy and productive approach to relationships, responsibilities, and personal growth as their child's journey through life.

Start Early: Begin setting boundaries when your child is young. This is an essential parenting practice that lays the groundwork for understanding limits and expectations. During the early years of development, children are like sponges, absorbing information and learning about the world around them. By establishing clear boundaries, parents provide a framework within which children can explore and interact safely. These boundaries offer a sense of security and structure, helping children grasp the concepts of acceptable behavior and personal responsibility. Consistent enforcement of these limits teaches children about consequences, promoting the development of self-discipline and respect for rules.

Setting rules for children is a fundamental aspect of parenting and caregiving that plays a pivotal role in their overall development. This chapter explores the importance of establishing rules, the principles behind effective rule-setting, and strategies for implementing rules that promote discipline, responsibility, and positive behavior in children.

Establishing clear and reasonable rules for children is crucial for their emotional, cognitive, and social development. Rules provide a foundation for children to learn the values, behaviors, and expectations of their family and society. They offer a sense of security and predictability, helping children navigate their world with confidence. Well-defined rules create a structured environment that fosters self-discipline, decision-making skills, and respect for boundaries.

Rules should be simple and easy to understand, using clear language appropriate for the child's age. Tailor the rules based on the child's developmental stage, considering their abilities and understanding. Encourage your child to take part in a rule to foster a sense of ownership and responsibility. Help children understand the reasons behind rules, enabling them to internalize the importance of following them. Emphasize rules that prioritize safety, health, and well-being. Try not to overwhelm your child. Avoid excessive rules and prioritize a few really important ones. Allow room for flexibility and adaptation when needed.

Be Clear and Specific: State the boundary explicitly and provide specific examples. For instance, instead of saying "Be good at the store," say "Stay close to me and don't touch things on the shelves."

Positive Framing: Frame boundaries positively. Instead of saying "Don't run indoors," say "Let's walk indoors to keep everyone safe."

Strong-willed children may resist rules. Maintaining open communication and explaining the reason and logic behind each rule is important. Showing what the consequences will be if they break the rule can also be helpful. We lived on a farm when our four children were little. They were involved in the care and breeding of all the animals. They learned early on that when the animals were breeding, they were having "sex" and that sex resulted in having a baby animal. Of course, I let them know that this applied to humans (animals) as well as their horses, sheep and cows.

During their early teenage years, I held concerns about the potential influence of less favorable companions on my children. I worried they might be introduced to unhealthful and dangerous substances. Coincidentally, the topic arose organically, prompting me to organize an enlightening trip to a hospital. They saw firsthand the consequences that infants face when exposed to drugs or substance abuse while in the womb. Compassionate pediatric nurses shared poignant tales of the infants under their care because of their parents' addictive behaviors, offering valuable insights. This experience left an enduring impression on my kids.

Modeling the behavior you wish to see in your children is of utmost importance. Your actions should align with your expectations. For instance, if you're aiming for them not to smoke, it's essential that you refrain from smoking yourself. Likewise, fostering a preference for healthy eating means avoiding the introduction of chips and cookies at home. Civil behavior hinges on avoiding yelling matches with your partner or with them. Encouraging openness and honesty mandates that you don't withhold secrets. When facing financial difficulties, it is beneficial to involve children, as it helps them learn to economize and prepares them to handle monetary stress when they face similar challenges as adults.

Offering explanations for the "Why" behind rules and expectations is a pivotal strategy in aiding children's comprehension. This approach empowers them to grasp the rationale underpinning these guidelines, allowing them to embrace their significance on a deeper level. Particularly with strong-willed children, who thrive on autonomy, providing structure intertwined with logical reasons is key. This not only aids in tempering defiance but also nurtures their cognitive development, as they internalize the connections between actions and their underlying meanings.

Establishing clear and appropriate consequences for rule-breaking is a fundamental aspect of effective discipline. By defining consequences that are directly linked to the misbehavior, children can better understand the cause-and-effect relationship between their actions and outcomes. This approach not only helps in teaching accountability but also provides a sense of fairness. When the rule violation leads to direct consequences, children are more likely to understand the purpose of the rule and the significance of following it. It's crucial to ensure that consequences are reasonable, proportional, and designed to encourage learning and growth rather than simply punishment.

Maintaining consistent enforcement of rules plays a pivotal role in guiding children's understanding of expectations and consequences. Consistent rule enforcement by parents or teachers enables children to comprehend what is expected of them, creating a stable and secure environment. This uniformity reinforces the idea that rules are not arbitrary but a set of guiding principles to ensure harmony and cooperation. Consistency becomes even more powerful when extended across all caregivers and various environments, as it establishes a unified framework for behavior. Whether at home, school, or other settings, the steady application of rules sends a coherent message, promoting a deeper comprehension of responsibility and accountability in children's minds.

Setting achievable goals is a pivotal strategy that fosters success and nurtures confidence. By defining objectives that are within reach, individuals are more likely to experience a sense of accomplishment, which bolsters their self-assurance. These attainable goals act as steppingstones, allowing for incremental progress and a tangible sense of growth. When individuals consistently meet these goals, they reinforce their belief in their capabilities and develop a positive outlook on their abilities. This positive cycle of setting, attaining, and surpassing realistic goals not only encourages continued effort but also cultivates a resilient mindset that embraces challenges as opportunities for growth.

Embracing flexibility and adaptation is paramount for navigating the complexities of life. Allowing room for flexibility enables individuals to respond effectively to changing circumstances and unexpected challenges. It encourages a mindset that is open to new ideas, solutions, and approaches, fostering creativity and innovation. Just as a tree bends with the wind to avoid breaking, the ability to adapt ensures resilience and the capacity to thrive in dynamic environments. By acknowledging that plans may need to be changed, individuals can reduce stress, enhance problem-solving skills, and maintain a healthier outlook. This willingness to adapt not only enhances personal growth but also cultivates a sense of empowerment, as individuals become more adept at navigating life's ever-changing landscape.

It's essential to recognize and embrace the power of positive reinforcement by rewarding and acknowledging adherence to rules. By doing so, we create a motivating environment that celebrates the effort and commitment individuals put into following guidelines. These rewards can be as simple as verbal praise or more tangible incentives, such as privileges or small treats.

This practice not only strengthens the connection between good behavior and positive outcomes, but also cultivates a sense of pride and accomplishment. By offering incentives, such as privileges or small treats, individuals are encouraged to make constructive choices more consistently, which strengthens the connection between good behavior and positive outcomes and cultivates a sense of pride and accomplishment.

Providing a selection of limited choices within the framework of established rules is a strategic way to foster autonomy and enhance decision-making skills. By offering options that align with the boundaries set by rules, it empowers individuals to exercise their judgment while staying within responsible boundaries.

This approach encourages a sense of ownership over decisions and actions, promoting a deeper understanding of consequences. It also nurtures the development of critical thinking as individuals learn to evaluate alternatives and make choices that align with their goals and values. As a result, this practice not only promotes a sense of independence but also equips individuals with valuable life skills that extend beyond the specific situation at hand.

Regularly reviewing and adjusting rules as children grow is a crucial aspect of effective parenting and guidance. As children develop, their needs, capabilities, and responsibilities strengthen. By revisiting and refining the rules, we ensure they remain relevant and supportive of their changing circumstances.

This adaptability reflects a commitment to nurturing their development, allowing rules to serve as a framework for growth rather than a static set of restrictions. By tailoring rules to each child's unique journey, we provide them with the tools to navigate their expanding world responsibly and ethically. This ongoing dialogue about rules and expectations not only deepens the parent-child connection, but also fosters a sense of mutual respect and understanding, laying the foundation for a healthy and positive upbringing.

Above all, it's essential to avoid the temptation of resorting to the phrase "because I said so." While it might provide a quick resolution to a situation, it misses a valuable opportunity for meaningful communication and understanding. Instead of fostering comprehension, this phrase can breed frustration and discourage children from questioning or learning the underlying reasons for rules.

By explaining the rationale behind the rules, we cultivate a sense of respect and empowerment within children, as they gain insights into the purpose and significance of guidelines. When we have open discussions about rules, we not only encourage critical thinking but also show children we value their thoughts and perspectives. Ultimately, this approach nurtures a foundation of trust, mutual respect, and shared responsibility between parents and children.

Setting clear boundaries with children is essential for their development and for maintaining a healthy parent-child relationship. Setting effective rules for children is a foundational aspect of parenting that helps guide their development into responsible, disciplined, and empathetic individuals. By adhering to the principles of clarity, consistency, age-appropriateness, and positive reinforcement, caregivers can create a supportive environment that nurtures children's growth while promoting positive behavior and values.

CHAPTER 2

CONSISTENCY IS KEY

Consistency plays a crucial role in helping children develop emotional security by providing a stable and predictable environment that contributes to a child's development and well-being.. Consistency helps children feel secure and safe. This emotional security refers to a child's confidence in their caregivers' availability, responsiveness, and support. When they know what to expect from their environment and caregivers, they are better able to develop a sense of trust and emotional stability.

Consistency in daily routines, such as mealtimes, bedtime, and playtime, provides a sense of order and structure that children can rely on. Consistency supports learning and cognitive development. When children experience consistent rules and expectations, they can better understand cause-and-effect relationships and develop problem-solving skills. Ultimately predictable routines and expectations help children understand the world around them.

Consistency in caregiving plays a pivotal role in nurturing a robust bond between children and their caregivers. When children receive unwavering love, attention, and responsiveness, they form a sense of security that lays the foundation for healthy emotional development. The predictability of consistent care enables children to develop trust, as they learn someone will consistently meet their needs. This influences the establishment of secure attachment styles, promoting emotional well-being and resilience. Caregiver consistency not only fosters a sense of stability and comfort, it also paves the way for children to form meaningful relationships, manage emotions, and navigate life's challenges with greater confidence.

Consistency in discipline and consequences is a cornerstone of effective parenting, as it provides children with a clear understanding of the boundaries surrounding acceptable behavior. When rules and consequences remain steady over time, children internalize the cause-and-effect relationship between their actions and outcomes. This understanding empowers them to develop self-control, as they recognize the potential consequences before making choices. Clear and consistent consequences not only deter undesirable behavior but also teach valuable life lessons in responsibility and accountability. Through this approach, children learn that their decisions have real-world repercussions, fostering the growth of thoughtful decision-making skills that extend into their adult lives.

Consistent interactions with both peers and adults play a pivotal role in shaping a child's social development. Regular engagement in social contexts offers children opportunities to practice communication, empathy, and cooperation. When they encounter predictable responses from others, they gain a better understanding of social dynamics and norms. This understanding empowers them to navigate social situations with confidence, as they become more adept at interpreting cues and responding appropriately. Through these consistent interactions, children refine their social skills, building the foundation for meaningful relationships and effective communication throughout their lives.

Consistency serves as a powerful catalyst for fostering children's exploration and independence. By offering predictable outcomes for their actions, children develop a sense of understanding and control over their environment. This predictability empowers them with the confidence to venture into new experiences, try different activities, and learn new skills. As they witness the cause-and-effect relationships through consistent responses, they become more willing to take initiative and make decisions on their own. This sense of mastery propels their growth and encourages them to embrace challenges, ultimately nurturing a foundation of self-assuredness that supports their journey toward independence.

An inconsistent environment can exert significant emotional strain on children, potentially leading to heightened stress and anxiety. When routines and responses vary unpredictably, children may struggle to establish a sense of stability and security. The lack of logical patterns can induce feelings of uncertainty, leaving them constantly on edge as they navigate an ever-changing landscape. This instability can impede their ability to concentrate, hinder their emotional regulation, and compromise their overall well-being. A consistent environment provides a reliable framework in which children can develop and flourish.

Knowing what to expect within a consistent environment is pivotal for children's emotional development and resilience. Predictability promotes a sense of safety that helps children expect outcomes and navigate difficult situations with greater preparedness. With consistent routines and responses, they can develop coping strategies and a stronger emotional foundation. When faced with difficulties, they can draw upon their previous experiences in similar circumstances, building their confidence in managing adversity. By reducing the uncertainties in their surroundings, children are better equipped to develop healthy emotional regulation and adapt to changes, ultimately fostering a sense of stability and confidence in their lives.

Consistency in communication is a fundamental driver in optimizing children's language acquisition. When caregivers consistently respond to a child's cues and employ consistent language patterns, children can more effectively grasp the nuances of communication. This predictability helps them associate specific words with corresponding actions or objects, accelerating their language development. The repetition and consistency of phrases aid in cementing vocabulary and sentence structures in their growing linguistic repertoire.

Beyond language, past experiences of consistency hold profound implications for a child's broader developmental trajectory. The stable and reliable communication patterns experienced in childhood can significantly influence their emotional and psychological growth. Such predictability fosters a sense of security and stability, contributing to the cultivation of resilience and a positive self-image. As children learn to navigate a world that responds to them consistently, they internalize a foundation of trust and emotional well-being that can extend far into their future endeavors.

While consistency undeniably holds value in guiding a child's development, it's imperative to recognize that it doesn't equate to an environment of unyielding control. Flexibility within a consistent framework allows children to explore, learn, and develop their own unique identities. Balancing predictability and adaptability nurtures their autonomy and creativity. Allowing room for spontaneity and individual expression within the parameters of consistent routines and expectations ensures children can flourish both within a stable foundation and amidst the diverse experiences that shape their growth.

Flexibility acts as an essential complement to consistency, allowing children to skillfully navigate new situations and embrace new experiences. In a rapidly changing world, the ability to adapt is essential, and children who possess this skill are better prepared for life's challenges. By finding the equilibrium between maintaining consistent structures and embracing occasional changes, caregivers foster an environment that seamlessly merges stability with adaptability. Encouraging this balanced approach helps children build resilience, problem-solving skills, and adaptability, enabling them to explore the world with confidence while still feeling secure with the consistency of support.

Consistency emerges as a pivotal force in nurturing comprehensive child development. By reviewing the list, it's apparent that consistency contributes to emotional security in children. It paves the way for stability and predictability in their lives, enabling them to comprehend rules, consequences, and social expectations. This sense of reliability empowers them to explore their environment, building both independence and resilience. Providing children with consistent communication and supportive boundaries leads to the development of strong linguistic skills and a solid foundation for emotional well-being. In sum, consistency stands as a cornerstone in the multifaceted journey of childhood development, offering a bedrock of security upon which children can flourish.

SUMMARY

Predictability: Children thrive when they know what to expect from their environment and caregivers. Consistent routines, schedules, and reactions to their emotions help children anticipate what will happen next. This predictability reduces feelings of anxiety and uncertainty, leading to a sense of emotional security.

Trust: Consistency in caregivers' responses builds trust. When caregivers consistently meet a child's emotional needs, such as offering comfort when the child is upset, the child learns their feelings are valid and that they can rely on their caregivers for support.

Attachment: Emotional security depends on a healthy attachment between a child and their caregivers. Consistency in nurturing, attention, and responsiveness fosters a strong emotional bond, enabling the child to feel secure and loved.

Emotional Regulation: Children learn how to manage their emotions by observing how caregivers respond to their own emotions and by experiencing consistent emotional support. When caregivers consistently provide comfort and guidance, children learn to regulate their emotions more effectively.

Sense of Belonging: A consistent and predictable environment helps children feel they belong. When they know they are cared for and that their needs will be met, they feel a sense of belonging and acceptance within their family.

Exploration and Independence: When children feel emotionally secure, they are more likely to explore their surroundings and try new experiences. They know they have a safe base to return to if things become overwhelming or unfamiliar.

Resilience: Consistency helps children develop resilience—the ability to bounce back from challenges. Emotional security enables children to navigate difficult situations knowing that they have a stable support system.

Confidence: Emotional security encourages children to develop a positive self-image. When caregivers consistently provide praise, encouragement, and positive reinforcement, children gain confidence in their abilities and self-worth.

Healthy Relationships: Children learn about healthy relationships from their interactions with caregivers. Consistent and nurturing relationships serve as models for how to engage with others, fostering positive social interactions.

Reduced Anxiety: Inconsistent or unpredictable environments can lead to anxiety in children. Consistency helps reduce anxiety by creating a reliable and safe framework within which children can explore and grow.

In summary, we foster emotional security through consistent caregiving, predictable routines, and responsive interactions. When children feel emotionally secure, they develop a firm foundation for healthy emotional, cognitive, and social development, setting the stage for well-being throughout their lives.

CHAPTER 3

HOW TO OFFER CHOICES

Offering choices to strong-willed children can be an effective way to harness their independent nature while maintaining a sense of structure and guidance. By providing opportunities for decision-making, parents can empower these children to exercise their autonomy in a controlled and productive manner. To effectively offer choices, consider the following strategies.

First, it's important to present choices that are age appropriate and relevant to the situation. Tailoring choices to their developmental stage ensures that the decisions they make are within their capacity to comprehend and manage. For example, a younger child might choose between two outfits for the day, while an older child could decide between completing homework before or after dinner.

Second, limit the number of options provided. While choices are empowering, too many options can overwhelm strong-willed children and lead to indecision or frustration. Presenting two or three viable alternatives allows them to decide more confidently. For instance, when selecting a weekend activity, offer a couple of options that align with their interests and your family's plans.

Third, ensure that the choices you offer are acceptable to you as a parent. While the goal is to empower your child, the options should all be suitable outcomes from your perspective. This maintains a sense of parental authority while still granting them a sense of control. For example, if you're deciding on a healthy snack, you could offer choices like apple slices or carrot sticks.

Involve strong-willed children in the decision-making process by discussing the potential outcomes of each choice. This encourages critical thinking and helps them learn to consider consequences before deciding. For instance, if they're choosing an extracurricular activity, discuss the time commitment, responsibilities, and potential benefits of each option.

Foster a sense of ownership by allowing them to follow through on their chosen course of action. If they've selected a particular chore to complete, hold them accountable for completing it. This not only teaches them responsibility but also shows that their decisions have real-world implications.

Lastly, be patient and supportive throughout the process. Strong-willed children may take longer to decide, and there will be times when they make choices that lead to less desirable outcomes. Use these moments as opportunities for learning rather than moments of criticism. Encourage them to reflect on their decisions and consider alternative approaches in the future.

Offering choices to strong-willed children is about striking a balance between fostering their independence and guiding them toward responsible decision-making. By tailoring choices, providing manageable options, maintaining parental boundaries, involving them in discussions, promoting accountability, and approaching the process with patience, parents can help these children develop essential life skills while nurturing their unique strengths.

Offering choices to children is a great way to give them a sense of autonomy and control, while still guiding their behavior within acceptable boundaries. Here's how you can effectively offer choices to children:

Provide Limited Options: Offering a restricted array of choices emerges as a strategic approach to prevent overwhelming children. By presenting a concise selection of options, typically ranging from two to three, caregivers can create a manageable decision-making process. This method ensures that we do not burden children with an excessive number of alternatives, allowing them to make decisions more confidently and efficiently. This practice not only streamlines the decision-making experience but also empowers children to exercise their autonomy while still benefiting from guidance and structure.

Make Both Options Acceptable: When presenting options, it's crucial to ensure that both alternatives are agreeable to you as a parent or caregiver. This approach guarantees that you're comfortable with either choice the child selects. By offering options that are within your realm of approval, you maintain a sense of control over the outcomes while still granting the child a degree of autonomy. This strategy not only fosters a constructive decision-making process, but also reinforces a collaborative dynamic between you and the child. It also minimizes the potential for conflicts arising from undesirable choices, promoting a harmonious environment built on mutual respect and understanding.

Age-Appropriate Choices: Tailoring choices to align with the child's age and developmental stage is essential for effective decision-making guidance. It's crucial to recognize that younger children require simpler options that are aligned with their cognitive abilities and comprehension. These choices might involve selecting from a few basic alternatives that they can readily understand. Your offering might go something like this: "Do you want an apple or a banana for your snack?" Or, "Would you like to wear the red shirt or the blue shirt today?"

Conversely, older children are more equipped to handle more intricate decisions that reflect their expanding capabilities. Here are two examples of choices involving more complex alternatives suitable for older children: "Would you prefer to work on your science project or read a chapter from your book?" Or, "Do you want to join the chess club or take part in the art workshop after school?" By offering choices that match their developmental milestones, caregivers ensure that the decision-making process is both meaningful and manageable for the child. This practice not only cultivates a sense of competence and responsibility but also promotes a healthy progression of decision-making skills throughout the child's growth journey.

Empower Them: Phrase the choices in an empowering manner. For example, instead of saying "Put on your coat," say "Would you like to wear your blue coat or your red coat today?" "Would you like to start your homework right after school or have a short break and then start?" "You have a choice between cleaning your room today or helping with setting the table for dinner. Which one would you prefer?"

Offer Visual Cues: For younger children or those who may struggle with verbal choices, you can use visual cues like pictures or objects representing the options. For example, you can use picture cards depicting options such as a picture of an apple and a picture of a banana to let the child choose their snack. You can assign colors to different choices like red for reading and blue for playing, and show the child the corresponding color to show their options. You can create a visual schedule with images representing activities like drawing, playing with toys and eating. Let the child point to the activity they'd like to do next.

Respect Their Decision: Once the child makes a choice, respect it. Respecting a child's decision after they've made a choice holds immense significance in nurturing their self-esteem and autonomy. Honoring the choice a child makes sends a powerful message that their opinions and decisions are valued. This validation reinforces their sense of agency and encourages them to take ownership of their choices. By consistently showing respect for their decisions, caregivers contribute to the development of confident decision-makers who are unafraid to express their preferences and navigate their world with conviction.

Highlight Positives: If one choice is more beneficial or preferred by you, highlight the positive aspects of that choice without making the other option seem negative. When navigating decision-making with children, emphasizing the positives of a particular choice, while refraining from portraying the alternative negatively, is a nuanced approach that can guide them towards favorable options without undue influence.

By highlighting the benefits of a preferred choice, caregivers provide valuable insights that enable children to make informed decisions. This technique encourages thoughtful consideration without imposing judgment on the other option. In doing so, they empower children to weigh their choices based on constructive information, fostering independent thought and a balanced perspective. This approach not only promotes sound decision-making, but also nurtures open communication and mutual respect between caregivers and children.

Encourage Independence: Choices should align with encouraging the child's independence and development. For example, allowing them to choose their outfit promotes decision-making skills. Encouraging independence through guided choices is a pivotal aspect of fostering a child's growth and development. Selecting choices that align with their increasing autonomy nurtures their decision-making skills while supporting their evolving sense of self.

An example of this is granting them the autonomy to choose their own outfit. By making decisions about their appearance, children learn to express their preferences, cultivate their personal style, and manage tasks on their own. This practice not only empowers them to take ownership of their choices but also builds their confidence, promoting a positive self-image and a strong sense of identity. Through such opportunities, caregivers play a vital role in nurturing a foundation of self-assurance and independence that extends well beyond the immediate decision at hand.

Practice Patience: Exercising patience is paramount when guiding children through decision-making processes, recognizing that they might require time to deliberate. In these moments, allowing space for their thought processes to unfold fosters a sense of respect for their autonomy. By practicing patience, caregivers send a message that their choices are valued and that their comfort and understanding are prioritized. This approach creates an environment where children feel unpressured and at ease, facilitating thoughtful decision-making. Through patient guidance, caregivers not only enable children to make informed choices but also demonstrate a foundational lesson in empathy and consideration for others.

Variety of Contexts: Presenting choices across a diverse range of contexts, spanning from meal selections to weekend activity decisions, is a strategic approach to nurturing well-rounded decision-making skills in children. By exposing them to different scenarios, caregivers encourage the development of flexible thinking. Making choices in various situations hones their ability to assess options, anticipate outcomes, and consider their personal preferences. This practice not only equips children with practical decision-making abilities, but also instills confidence in their capacity to navigate a wide array of life's choices. As they gain experience across diverse contexts, children become better equipped to make informed decisions and embrace the challenges and opportunities that present themselves throughout their lives.

Here is a list of diverse questions:

Meal Choices: "Would you like pasta or chicken for dinner tonight?"

Playtime Activities: "Do you want to build with blocks or play with puzzles?"

Weekend Outings: "Do you want to go to the park or the zoo this weekend?"

Bedtime Routine: "Would you like to read a book or have a bedtime story?"

Clothing Selection: "Do you want to wear your red shoes or your blue shoes today?"

Homework Schedule: "Would you like to finish math first or work on your reading assignment?"

Arts and Crafts: "Do you want to paint or do some crafting with clay?"

After-School Snack: "Would you like an apple or a banana for your snack?"

Free Time Activities: "Do you want to ride your bike or play a board game?"

Outdoor Play: "Do you want to kick a ball around or fly a kite at the park?"

Model Decision Making: Share your decision-making process with them sometimes. Narrate how you make choices and why you choose certain options. Modeling decision-making is a valuable strategy for helping children grasp the intricacies of making choices. By openly sharing one's own decision-making process, caregivers provide children with insights into the thoughtfulness and considerations that go into selecting options. Narrating the reasons behind specific choices not only demystifies decision-making but also encourages children to think critically about their own preferences and priorities.

This approach offers a practical learning experience, equipping children with a mental toolkit for assessing alternatives, anticipating consequences, and aligning choices with personal values. Through this interactive modeling, caregivers not only cultivate informed decision-makers but also foster a climate of open communication and shared problem-solving between generations.

Avoid Overusing Choices: While offering choices is a constructive and beneficial approach, avoid turning every situation into a choice. It's essential to exercise moderation and avoid transforming every scenario into a decision-making opportunity.

While choices empower children, some situations need clear directives without room for negotiation. Balancing the introduction of choices with moments of authoritative decision-making helps children learn the distinction between situations that allow flexibility and those that require compliance.

This practice cultivates an understanding of responsibility and authority while preserving the value of choices in the right contexts. Striking this equilibrium ensures that children learn to respect rules and also appreciate the freedom that comes with thoughtful decision-making. Some decisions need to be made without negotiation.

Offer "No" as a Choice: In certain situations, you can offer a "no" option as well. In specific scenarios, it's valuable to include a "no" option among the choices offered to children. Acknowledging "no" as a valid choice respects their autonomy and preferences while fostering a sense of empowerment. This approach reinforces the idea that we respect their feelings and boundaries, promoting healthy communication and self-advocacy. While it might not always be workable, incorporating the "no" option when appropriate empowers children to assert themselves within the decision-making process, ultimately contributing to their development of assertiveness and a strong sense of agency.

Teaching children they can express "no" when appropriate is a fundamental aspect of their personal development and boundary-setting skills. Encouraging them to use this word helps them understand their autonomy and develop a sense of agency over their choices and interactions. It empowers them to voice their feelings, preferences, and limitations in situations where they may feel uncomfortable or unsafe.

Offering "no" as a choice also establishes a foundation for open communication and mutual respect, both within their relationships with caregivers and as they interact with peers. It's a valuable life skill that teaches children the importance of assertiveness and establishes the boundaries necessary for their emotional well-being and personal growth.

Encourage Problem Solving: When confronted with challenges, inviting a child's input on how to navigate the situation serves as a catalyst for honing their problem-solving abilities. By seeking their perspective, caregivers encourage children to think critically and creatively about solutions. This collaborative approach not only enables them to take an active part in discovering solutions but also cultivates a feeling of responsibility for the results. Through this practice, children learn to assess situations, weigh alternatives, and make informed decisions, all of which are essential life skills. This method not only equips them to tackle immediate challenges but also instills a mindset of resilience and resourcefulness that extends into their future endeavors.

Acknowledge Their Preferences: It's important to recognize the value of a child's choices and preferences, even if you can't always give them what they want. Acknowledging the value of a child's choices and preferences, even when accommodation isn't always possible, is a pivotal aspect of nurturing their self-esteem and self-worth. By demonstrating that their opinions matter, caregivers create an environment where children feel respected and understood.

This practice not only strengthens the parent-child bond but also cultivates a sense of validation that contributes to their overall emotional well-being. It teaches children that their voices hold weight, fostering a foundation of confidence that empowers them to communicate openly and assertively in various life contexts. Ultimately, the act of valuing their choices, irrespective of the outcome, leaves a lasting impression on children's perception of their significance and their place within their familial and social spheres.

Gradually Increase Complexity: As children progress in their development, progressively introducing more intricate choices enables them to refine their decision-making abilities across a spectrum of scenarios. Gradually expanding the complexity of choices aligns with their expanding reasoning and emotional capacities, encouraging them to think critically and weigh options in a nuanced manner.

This approach not only cultivates adaptable problem-solving skills but also instills the confidence to handle diverse challenges. By gradually challenging them with more multifaceted decisions, caregivers equip children with a robust toolkit for navigating the complexities of the world, fostering independence and self-assuredness.

Remember that offering choices should be a positive experience that fosters independence and responsibility. It's a tool for helping children learn to make decisions, while still operating within the boundaries you've established as a parent or caregiver.

Here are some examples of how you can offer choices to children in various situations:

Mealtime Choices:

"Do you want to have spaghetti or chicken for dinner tonight?"

"Would you like apples or bananas as a snack?"

"Do you prefer milk or juice with your breakfast?"

Getting Dressed:

"Do you want to wear the blue shirt or the red shirt today?"

"Would you like to wear shorts or pants?"

"Do you want to put on your shoes before or after your socks?"

Playtime Choices:

> "Would you like to play with blocks or puzzles?"
>
> "Do you want to play outside or do an indoor activity?"
>
> "Would you like to play with your trains or your dolls?"

Bedtime Routine:

> "Do you want to brush your teeth first or put on your pajamas?"
>
> "Would you like to read two short stories or one longer story before bed?"
>
> "Do you want your teddy bear or your stuffed elephant to sleep with tonight?"

Homework or Chores:

> "Do you want to start with math homework or reading?"
>
> "Would you like to clean up your toys before or after you finish your snack?"

Weekend Activities:

> "Do you want to go to the park or the zoo this weekend?"
>
> "Would you like to bake cookies or go for a bike ride?"

Behavioral Choices:

> "Do you want to use your indoor voice or your whisper voice in the library?"
>
> "Would you like to clean up your toys now or in 10 minutes?"
>
> "Do you want to hold my hand while crossing the street or stay close by?"

Shopping Decisions:

> "Do you want the blue backpack or the green one for school?"
>
> "Would you like the strawberry yogurt or the vanilla yogurt?"

Art and Craft Time:

> "Do you want to use markers or crayons for your drawing?"
>
> "Would you like to make a collage or paint a picture?"

Weeknight Activities:

> "Do you want to do your music practice before or after dinner?"
>
> "Would you like to do a puzzle or build with Legos before bedtime?"

Remember, the goal is to offer choices that are age appropriate and relevant to the situation. Providing choices empowers children, helps them practice decision-making, and fosters their sense of independence while staying within the boundaries you've set as a parent or caregiver.

CHAPTER 4

EMPATHETIC LISTENING

Strong-willed children possess a unique and formidable spirit that, while challenging for parents, can ultimately foster remarkable growth and development. These children exhibit an unwavering determination and independence from an early age, often displaying an unyielding stance about their preferences, desires, and beliefs. While parenting such individuals can be a daunting task, it is undeniably crucial for parents to take a major role in guiding them through life's challenges, as this can significantly affect their journey toward becoming strong and significant adults.

One of the key aspects of nurturing strong-willed children is recognizing the potential within their spirited nature. Rather than attempting to suppress their innate tendencies, parents can help channel their energy in positive directions. By providing a supportive environment that encourages critical thinking, problem-solving, and self-expression, parents can mold these children into assertive and capable individuals who can stand up for themselves and their beliefs constructively.

Parents play a pivotal role in helping strong-willed children develop essential life skills such as empathy, effective communication, and conflict resolution. These skills are crucial for building healthy relationships and navigating the complexities of the adult world. By engaging in open conversations, actively listening to their concerns, and teaching them how to consider different perspectives, parents can equip their children with the tools they need to interact successfully with peers, colleagues, and authority figures.

Guiding strong-willed children also involves setting clear boundaries and expectations. This provides them with a sense of structure and discipline while allowing room for their independent nature to flourish. When parents establish consistent rules and consequences, it helps these children understand the importance of accountability and responsible decision-making. This guidance lays the foundation for them to become adults who can navigate ethical dilemmas and societal norms with confidence.

Parents have a significant impact on the self-esteem and self-worth of their strong-willed children, and this cannot be overstated. By providing unconditional love and acceptance, parents bolster their children's self-confidence, enabling them to embrace their uniqueness without fear of rejection. When parents acknowledge their achievements, no matter how small, and offer constructive feedback during setbacks, they instill a resilient mindset that is crucial for handling life's challenges with grace and determination.

The journey of strong-willed children toward becoming significant adults is a partnership between their inherent nature and the guidance provided by their parents. With the right approach, parents can harness the power of their child's determination, shaping it into a force that drives personal growth, resilience, and positive contributions to society. By embracing their role as mentors, supporters, and advocates, parents pave the way for these spirited individuals to emerge as strong, influential adults capable of making meaningful contributions to the world.

Being an empathetic listener to your strong-willed child is a crucial aspect of fostering a healthy parent-child relationship and helping them navigate the world effectively. Here are some strategies to become a more empathetic listener:

First, create a comfortable and non-judgmental environment where your child feels safe expressing their thoughts and feelings. Let them know you are genuinely interested in what they have to say and that their emotions are valid. This open atmosphere encourages them to open up and share their thoughts with you.

Practice active listening by giving your full attention when your child speaks. Put away distractions, make eye contact, and show that you are fully engaged in the conversation. Nodding or offering occasional affirmations can show that you're following along and encouraging them to continue sharing.

Validate their emotions and experiences. Even if you don't always agree with their perspective, acknowledging their feelings shows you respect their individuality. Phrases like "I can understand why you feel that way" or "It sounds like you're really frustrated" can help them feel understood.

Avoid immediately offering solutions or advice. Sometimes, strong-willed children simply need to express themselves without seeking a fix. Instead of jumping in with solutions, ask if they would like your input or if they're looking for advice. This empowers them to decide what level of support they need.

Repeat what the child said to make sure you have understood correctly. Summarize their feelings and thoughts, giving them the opportunity to clarify or elaborate. This shows that you're genuinely trying to comprehend their perspective.

Practice patience and give them the time they need to express themselves fully. Strong-willed children might take their time in sharing their thoughts. Trying to interrupt their thoughts before they can express them, or rushing the conversation can shut down their willingness to communicate openly.

Being an empathetic listener to your strong-willed child involves creating a safe space, practicing active listening, validating their emotions, withholding immediate advice, reflecting on what you've heard, and exercising patience. These strategies not only strengthen your relationship but also empower your child to develop effective communication skills and a sense of being heard and understood.

Here are some examples of how you can be an empathetic listener to a strong-willed child:

Validation of Emotions:

Child: "I don't want to go to school today! I hate it!"

Parent: "It sounds like you're feeling really unhappy about going to school. Can you tell me more about what's bothering you?"

Reflecting Feelings:

Child: "I don't want to share my toys with my sister! She always breaks them!"

Parent: "It seems like you're frustrated because you're worried your toys might get broken. Is that how you're feeling?"

Open-Ended Questions:

Child: "I don't like my new teacher. She's so strict."

Parent: "Tell me more about what you find strict about the new teacher. What specific things are bothering you?"

Avoiding Immediate Solutions:

Child: "I don't understand this math problem, and I'm stuck!"

Parent: "I see you're having trouble with this math problem. Would you like me to help you work through it together, or would you prefer to figure it out on your own?"

Summarizing:

Child: "I had a fight with my friend today. She took my crayons without asking."

Parent: "So, your friend took your crayons without asking, and that made you upset. Is that right?"

Patient Listening:

Child: (after a long pause) "I don't really know if I want to join the soccer team."

Parent: "It's okay if you're unsure about joining the soccer team. Take your time. I'm here to listen whenever you're ready to talk about it."

Offering Support:

Child: "I'm scared of the dark and I can't sleep at night."

Parent: "I understand that the dark can be scary sometimes. Would you like to keep a nightlight on, or maybe we can find another way to help you feel more comfortable?"

Empathetic Responses:

Child: "I failed the science test, and I'm really disappointed in myself."

Parent: "I can see how disappointed you are about the test. It's okay to feel upset, and we can work together to figure out how to improve next time."

In each of these examples, the parent shows empathetic listening by acknowledging the child's emotions, reflecting back their feelings, asking open-ended questions, avoiding jumping to solutions, summarizing their thoughts, showing patience, and offering support. These responses help the strong-willed child feel heard, understood, and valued, ultimately fostering a stronger parent-child connection and aiding the child's emotional growth.

CHAPTER 5

ENCOURAGE INDEPENDENCE

Fostering independence in strong-willed children is an essential aspect of nurturing their growth and preparing them for the challenges of the future. These spirited individuals possess a natural drive to assert their autonomy, and harnessing this inclination can lead to remarkable personal development.

Encouraging independence in such children goes beyond mere self-sufficiency; it instills a sense of responsibility, critical thinking, and resilience that will serve them well as they navigate the complexities of adulthood. By providing opportunities for decision-making, problem-solving, and taking ownership of their actions, parents and caregivers play a vital role in shaping strong-willed children into self-assured, capable individuals ready to make meaningful contributions to the world.

The journey of encouraging independence is rooted in recognizing and honoring the unique qualities of strong-willed children. These individuals exhibit a remarkable determination and passion from a young age, demonstrating a tenacity that, when nurtured correctly, can develop into a powerful force for positive change.

However, this path requires a delicate balance between guidance and autonomy. Parents must provide a supportive framework that allows room for exploration while offering guidance to help them channel their energy effectively. By striking this balance, parents empower their strong-willed children to become self-starters who approach challenges with enthusiasm and an innate belief in their capabilities.

The importance of encouraging independence in strong-willed children extends beyond their personal growth; it contributes to building a resilient and adaptable society. As these children mature into adults who value and understand their individuality, they become more likely to challenge societal norms, advocate for change, and pursue innovative solutions to complex problems.

By nurturing their ability to think critically, make choices, and learn from both successes and failures, parents prepare them to take on leadership roles and make meaningful contributions to their communities. In a world that increasingly requires individuals to navigate ambiguity and embrace change, fostering independence in strong-willed children is an investment not only in their future but in the betterment of society.

Encouraging independence in a strong-willed child is a valuable approach that can nurture their self-confidence, decision-making skills, and sense of responsibility. Here are some effective strategies along with examples:

Provide Age-Appropriate Tasks: Assign tasks that align with their capabilities and age. For instance, you can ask a younger child to choose their own clothes for the day or let them decide which book to read before bedtime. For older children, you might involve them in planning a family outing or allow them to manage their school assignments independently.

Here are some specific examples of age-appropriate tasks for children and adolescents:

Preschoolers (Ages 3-5):

- Sorting and matching objects by color, shape, or size.
- Putting away toys and books after playtime.

Simple chores like dusting low surfaces or feeding a pet with supervision.

Dressing themselves with minimal assistance.

Watering plants with a small watering can.

Early Elementary School (Ages 6-8):

Setting the table for meals.

Helping prepare simple snacks, like spreading peanut butter on bread.

Folding and putting away laundry (socks, t-shirts).

Keeping their room tidy, making their bed.

Taking responsibility for a small pet's basic care (e.g., filling a water dish).

Late Elementary School (Ages 9-11):

Packing their own school bag and making sure they have the necessary materials.

Assisting with meal preparation under supervision (e.g., chopping vegetables).

Helping with grocery shopping by making a list or finding items in the store.

Managing their own daily schedule and homework assignments.

Raking leaves or shoveling snow with proper guidance and equipment.

Middle School (Ages 12-14):

Doing their own laundry from start to finish.

Cooking simple meals independently (e.g., pasta dishes).

Babysitting younger siblings for short periods under adult supervision.

Managing an allowance or budget for personal expenses.

Volunteering for community service projects.

High School (Ages 15-17):

Maintaining a part-time job and managing their earnings.

Planning and cooking a family meal on their own.

Taking public transportation or driving to school and extracurricular activities.

Managing their own online presence responsibly and with privacy in mind.

Assisting with more complex household chores like mowing the lawn or deep cleaning.

Late High School (Ages 18+):

Completing college applications and financial aid forms.

Managing personal finances, including banking, budgeting, and paying bills.

Taking on more significant responsibilities within the household, such as grocery shopping and meal planning.

Learning basic home maintenance skills like changing a tire or fixing a leaky faucet.

Pursuing part-time jobs or internships in line with career interests.

Offer Choices

Give them options within limits. For example, when preparing meals, offer a choice between two healthy sides. This lets them make a decision while still adhering to guidelines. I know I covered this in Chapter 3, but here's a recap of that.

Offering choices within limits is a crucial aspect of fostering independence and decision-making skills in children while maintaining a structured and safe environment. This approach acknowledges the developmental stage of the child and encourages them to exercise autonomy within predefined boundaries. It recognizes that children have unique preferences and ideas, which can contribute to their overall development.

When implementing choices within limits, parents and caregivers should consider age-appropriate options that align with the child's capabilities and understanding. For example, we might give a toddler a choice between two outfits to wear for the day, promoting a sense of control over their appearance without overwhelming them with too many options.

As children grow, the choices can become more complex, such as selecting extracurricular activities or deciding on weekend plans. Setting limits within these choices is essential to ensure safety and adherence to family values. For instance, a teenager may have the choice of which after-school activity to take part in, but still within the limit that it doesn't interfere with academic responsibilities or violate household rules.

Offering choices within limits not only empowers children to make decisions but also helps them develop critical thinking and problem-solving skills. It encourages them to consider consequences, weigh options, and learn from their choices. This approach can reduce power struggles and enhance the parent-child relationship by promoting mutual respect and open communication.

It's important for parents and caregivers to maintain consistency in setting and enforcing limits, as this provides a stable framework within which children can explore their autonomy and gradually develop a sense of responsibility and self-discipline. Ultimately, choices within limits contribute to a child's growth into a responsible, self-reliant, and confident individual.

Encourage Problem-Solving: Encouraging problem-solving skills in children offers a wide range of benefits that are crucial for their intellectual, emotional, and social development. Problem solving is a fundamental cognitive skill that stimulates a child's thinking abilities. It requires them to analyze a situation, identify potential solutions, and make decisions based on available information. By engaging in problem-solving activities, children enhance their critical thinking, logical reasoning, and analytical skills. These cognitive skills not only apply to academic tasks but also have real-world applications, helping children excel in various aspects of life, from school assignments to future career challenges.

Problem solving teaches children resilience and emotional regulation. When children face problems, they often experience frustration, disappointment, or even anxiety. However, by encouraging them to tackle these challenges, parents and caregivers help children develop emotional intelligence and coping mechanisms. As they encounter and overcome obstacles, children gain a sense of accomplishment and self-confidence. They learn that setbacks are a natural part of life and that they have the capability to confront and surmount difficulties. This, in turn, contributes to higher self-esteem and a more positive self-image, which can have long-lasting benefits for their mental well-being.

Problem-solving skills are essential for effective interpersonal relationships. When children engage in group activities or play with peers, they often encounter conflicts or disagreements. Learning how to negotiate, compromise, and find mutually agreeable solutions is vital for building positive relationships and resolving disputes constructively. Encouraging problem solving in a social context promotes teamwork, communication, and empathy, which are crucial for successful collaboration and conflict resolution throughout life. These social skills not only aid children in their interactions with peers but also lay the foundation for healthy relationships with family members, friends, and colleagues in adulthood.

Parents can provide their child with puzzles of increasing complexity as they grow. For instance, starting with simple jigsaw puzzles and gradually moving to more challenging ones. When the child encounters difficulty, the parent can guide them to break the problem down into smaller parts, discuss strategies for solving it, and encourage persistence. This not only enhances the child's spatial reasoning and problem-solving skills but also teaches them patience and the value of perseverance.

When a child faces difficulties with their homework or school projects, parents can act as facilitators rather than providing direct answers. They can ask questions to prompt critical thinking, such as "What do you understand from the question?" or "How do you think we can find the answer?" By guiding the child through the problem-solving process, parents help them develop research skills, learn how to access resources, and independently work through academic challenges. This approach instills a sense of responsibility and autonomy in their learning journey.

In situations where siblings or friends have conflicts, parents can encourage their child to find solutions rather than intervening immediately. For instance, if two siblings are fighting over a toy, the parent can suggest that they brainstorm ways to share it or take turns. By involving the child in finding a resolution, parents teach empathy, negotiation, and cooperation. They also reinforce the concept that peaceful resolution of conflicts through communication and compromise is possible.

Parents can involve children in real-life problem-solving situations. For example, if the family is planning a vacation, parents can discuss options and involve the child in choosing destinations, setting a budget, and creating an itinerary. This provides children with a practical understanding of decision-making, financial planning, and time management. Parents can motivate their children to take part in trip-related responsibilities, like packing their suitcase or researching activities at the destination, so that they feel included in the family's decisions.

In all these examples, the key is for parents to act as guides and facilitators, empowering their children to think critically, analyze problems, and come up with solutions independently. By providing support and encouraging an environment where problem-solving is promoted, parents can help their children develop cognitive skills, emotional growth, and social competence. These skills empower children to approach challenges with confidence, adaptability, and a positive mindset. Parents helping their children with problem solving not only help them develop valuable life skills that will serve them well throughout their lives, but also set them on a path toward success in both their personal and academic lives.

Supporting Responsibility: Encouraging responsibility in children fosters a sense of independence and self-efficacy. When parents give children tasks and responsibilities that are appropriate for their age, they teach them that they can take action and make a difference in their family or community. This sense of capability and autonomy is a vital component of healthy self-esteem and self-confidence. As children experience success in completing tasks and meeting their responsibilities, they develop a belief in their own abilities, which translates into a willingness to tackle new challenges and take on leadership roles later in life.

Responsibility is a foundational life skill that prepares children for the demands and responsibilities of adulthood. As children grow and eventually become independent, they will need to manage various aspects of their lives, including personal finances, household chores, and work responsibilities. By instilling a strong sense of responsibility early on, parents and caregivers equip children with the skills and mindset needed to navigate the complexities of adulthood successfully. This includes time management, organization, and accountability—skills that are valuable in both personal and professional contexts.

Responsibility is closely tied to moral and ethical values. When children are responsible, they learn to consider the consequences of their actions and make choices that align with their values and societal norms. This includes being accountable for their actions, respecting the rights and property of others, and understanding the importance of honesty and integrity. Nurturing these qualities from a young age helps children become responsible, ethical, and compassionate individuals who contribute positively to their communities.

Responsibility plays a pivotal role in developing healthy interpersonal relationships. When children understand the importance of fulfilling their obligations and meeting their commitments, they build trust and reliability in their relationships with family, friends, and peers. They are seen as dependable and considerate individuals, which fosters strong, lasting connections. The ability to collaborate and work responsibly in group settings is a valuable skill in school, sports, and extracurricular activities, setting children up for success in both social and academic contexts.

Supporting responsibility in children is crucial for their personal growth, preparation for adulthood, development of moral values, and building strong relationships. Parents, caregivers, and educators play a vital role in nurturing this essential quality by providing opportunities for children to take on responsibilities, learn from their experiences, and gradually become accountable, self-sufficient, and ethical individuals.

Here are six examples of how parents can support responsibility at different stages of childhood and adolescence:

Early Childhood (Ages 2-6):

Establish Routines: Create daily routines that include age-appropriate tasks like making the bed, cleaning up toys, or helping with simple meal preparation. Consistency in routines helps children understand their responsibilities.

Use Visual Aids: Use charts or visual schedules with pictures to help young children understand and follow their daily responsibilities. They can check off or move a picture as they complete each task, providing a sense of accomplishment.

Praise and Encouragement: Offer praise and positive reinforcement when children fulfill their responsibilities. This reinforces their motivation to continue helping with tasks.

Middle Childhood (Ages 7-11):

Chores and Contributions: Assign regular chores like doing dishes, folding laundry, or taking care of a family pet. Rotate responsibilities to teach various tasks and teamwork.

Homework Management: Encourage children to take responsibility for their schoolwork, such as organizing their backpack, completing assignments on time, and seeking help when needed.

Budgeting and Saving: Teach the basics of money management by providing an allowance and discussing saving, spending, and charitable giving. Encourage them to set financial goals and save for desired items.

Early Adolescence (Ages 12-14):

Time Management: Help adolescents develop time management skills by allowing them to manage their own schedules, including homework, extracurricular activities, and chores. Encourage them to use digital tools or planners.

Cooking and Meal Planning: Involve teenagers in meal planning and cooking. They can take responsibility for preparing family meals or their own snacks, promoting independence and nutrition awareness.

Conflict Resolution: Teach problem-solving and conflict resolution skills in interpersonal relationships. Encourage open communication and problem-solving strategies when disagreements arise with friends or family.

Late Adolescence (Ages 15-18):

Part-Time Jobs: Support teens in finding part-time jobs or internships, allowing them to experience workplace responsibilities and financial independence.

College and Career Preparation: Involve them in planning for college or career choices, including researching options, applying for scholarships, and managing application deadlines.

Independent Living Skills: Before leaving for college or moving out, ensure they have essential life skills such as budgeting, laundry, cooking, and basic home maintenance.

That was a simplified and brief overview. While I'll delve into each stage further, it's key to grasp that parents need to model responsibility, offer guidance and feedback, and raise expectations as children mature. Preparing children for a successful transition into adulthood requires the practice of open communication and setting realistic expectations that help them develop autonomy and responsibility.

As promised, here's the detailed information on the significance of each aspect of parenting steps.

Homework Management: Homework management is a critical skill that helps students become independent learners and develop valuable time management abilities. Allowing children to take charge of their homework routine by setting a designated study time and permitting them to decide the order of subjects can be highly beneficial.

First, giving children the responsibility to manage their homework routine teaches them valuable time management skills. When they have control over their study schedule, they learn how to allocate time efficiently for different subjects and assignments. They begin to understand the importance of pacing themselves, setting goals, and meeting deadlines. As they consistently apply these strategies, these skills become a natural part of their abilities. This skill is not only vital for academic success but also transfers to many aspects of life, from managing work tasks to organizing personal responsibilities.

Second, allowing children to choose the order in which they tackle subjects encourages them to take ownership of their learning process. It respects their individual learning preferences and style. Some children may prefer to start with their favorite subjects, while others may opt to tackle more challenging ones first. This autonomy fosters a sense of independence and self-awareness, as children learn what study methods work best for them. It also helps them develop problem-solving skills, as they may need to adjust their approach if they encounter difficulties with certain subjects.

This approach promotes responsibility and accountability. When children have a say in their homework routine, they are more likely to take ownership of their academic responsibilities. They learn that their choices have consequences, such as completing assignments on time or facing the consequences of procrastination. This understanding of accountability is a crucial life skill that extends beyond the classroom, teaching children the importance of following through with commitment and being responsible individuals.

Last, empowering children to prioritize and manage their workload effectively contributes to reduced stress and increased motivation. When they have control over their study time, they can adapt their schedule to align with their energy levels and extracurricular commitments. This can lead to a more balanced and less stressful academic experience, fostering a positive attitude towards learning. It also encourages children to take the initiative in seeking help or additional resources if needed, as they recognize the responsibility for their own academic success lies with them.

Allowing children to manage their homework routine by setting a designated study time and permitting them to decide the order of subjects is an effective way to promote time management, independence, responsibility, and motivation. Parents and educators can support this process by offering guidance, monitoring progress, and providing a supportive environment that encourages children to take charge of their own learning.

Personal Goals: Encouraging children to set personal goals is a valuable practice that can positively affect their development throughout various stages of childhood. Encourage them to set personal goals. Goal setting instills a sense of responsibility in children. When they set their own objectives, they take ownership of their actions and decisions. This fosters accountability, as they understand that they are responsible for the outcomes, whether positive or negative. Learning to set and achieve goals is a vital component of becoming a responsible and self-sufficient individual.

Goal setting encourages independence and self-determination. Children learn to think for themselves, make choices, and set priorities based on their own desires and aspirations. This autonomy is a crucial aspect of personal development and helps children become more self-reliant. Achieving personal goals boosts self-confidence. When children experience success in reaching their objectives, whether small or large, they develop a sense of accomplishment and belief in their abilities. This newfound confidence can spill over into other areas of their lives, motivating them to tackle more significant challenges.

Goal setting provides motivation and encourages persistence. When children have an obvious target, they are more likely to stay focused, work diligently, and persevere through challenges. The satisfaction of achieving their goals reinforces the idea that effort leads to success, which can inspire them to set and pursue new goals in various aspects of their lives. Setting goals also requires planning and organization. Children learn to break down larger objectives into smaller, manageable steps, creating a roadmap for their achievements. This process teaches them valuable skills in time management, prioritization, and task organization, which are beneficial not only academically but also in everyday life.

Goal setting encourages children to reflect on their values and aspirations. It prompts them to consider what truly matters to them and what they want to achieve in the short and long term. This self-reflection helps children develop a sense of purpose and direction, guiding them towards positive decision-making and personal growth. Goal setting empowers children by giving them a sense of control over their lives. In a world full of uncertainties, setting and pursuing personal goals can provide a reassuring sense of structure and direction. This feeling of control can reduce anxiety and stress, especially during times of change or transition.

The following breaks down personal goal ideas for different age ranges.

Early Childhood (Ages 2-6): During these formative years, setting simple personal goals can help children develop essential life skills and build confidence. These goals might involve basic tasks like dressing themselves or tying their shoelaces. As children achieve these small milestones, they gain a sense of accomplishment and independence. This early exposure to goal setting lays the foundation for more complex goals in later stages. Here are some more ideas for this age group.

Dressing Independently: Encourage your child to learn how to put on and take off simple clothing items like t-shirts, pants, and shoes.

Toileting: Support them in achieving bathroom independence, including using the toilet, washing hands, and flushing.

Feeding: Promote self-feeding with utensils, drinking from a cup, and learning table manners.

Sharing and Taking Turns: Teach your child the importance of sharing toys and taking turns during playtime, helping them develop social skills and patience.

Expressing Emotions: Encourage your child to express their feelings verbally, helping them identify and communicate emotions like happiness, frustration, or sadness.

Empathy: Foster empathy by discussing feelings and encouraging your child to understand and support the emotions of others.

Vocabulary Expansion: Introduce new words and concepts through reading and conversation, helping them build a strong vocabulary.

Storytelling: Encourage your child to tell simple stories or share their day's experiences, enhancing their language and communication skills.

Listening Skills: Promote active listening by engaging in conversations and asking questions, reinforcing the importance of listening to others.

Puzzle Solving: Offer age-appropriate puzzles and games to develop problem-solving and fine motor skills.

Counting and Recognizing Numbers: Introduce counting and basic number recognition through games, counting objects, or pointing out numbers in the environment. Don't wait for school to do your job.

Shapes and Colors: Help your child identify and name shapes and colors in everyday objects and activities.

Gross Motor Skills: Encourage physical activity and the development of gross motor skills through activities like running, jumping, and climbing.

Fine Motor Skills: Support the refinement of fine motor skills by engaging in activities like coloring, drawing, using scissors, or building with blocks.

Hand-Eye Coordination: Practice activities that involve hand-eye coordination, such as catching and throwing a ball or stacking objects.

Remember that these goals should be flexible and tailored to your child's individual needs and developmental stage. To make learning enjoyable for your child, introduce goals gradually and in a playful way that is appropriate for their age.

Middle Childhood (Ages 7-11): In this stage, children can begin setting academic and extracurricular goals. Encouraging them to set goals for reading a certain number of books, improving their math grades, or mastering a new skill such as playing a musical instrument, fosters a sense of responsibility and motivation. Achieving these goals reinforces their belief in their abilities and helps them understand the connection between effort and success.

Improved Reading Skills: Set a goal for your child to read a certain number of books or pages within a specific timeframe. This encourages a love for reading and enhances literacy.

Math Proficiency: Encourage your child to work on specific math skills, such as mastering multiplication tables or solving more complex word problems.

Homework Routine: Help your child establish a consistent homework routine, including setting aside dedicated time each day for studying and completing assignments.

Household Chores: Assign age-appropriate chores like making their bed daily, setting the table for meals, or helping with grocery shopping.

Time Management: Teach them to manage their time effectively by creating schedules for homework, chores, and extracurricular activities.

Self-Care: Promote personal responsibility by encouraging them to independently organize their belongings, keep their room tidy, and remember important dates and responsibilities.

Conflict Resolution: Teach problem-solving and conflict resolution skills, including how to express themselves calmly, listen actively, and find solutions in interpersonal conflicts.

Empathy and Friendship: Encourage your child to develop empathy by understanding and supporting the feelings of others. Set goals for making new friends or nurturing existing friendships.

Self-Expression: Help them find positive outlets for self-expression, such as journaling, art, or joining clubs or sports teams to explore their interests.

Physical Activity: Promote regular physical activity by setting goals for participation in sports, dance, or other physical activities they enjoy.

Healthy Eating: Encourage making nutritious food choices and setting goals related to trying new fruits and vegetables or packing a healthy school lunch.

Sleep Routine: Establish a consistent sleep routine to ensure your child gets enough rest for optimal physical and mental well-being.

Skill Development: Support your child in pursuing hobbies or interests they are passionate about, such as learning a musical instrument, painting, coding, or any other skill they wish to develop.

Extracurricular Involvement: Encourage them to explore extracurricular activities or clubs at school, setting goals related to participation and commitment.

Community Engagement: Foster a sense of responsibility toward the community by encouraging volunteer work or taking part in community service projects.

These goals should be age-appropriate, flexible, and tailored to your child's interests and developmental stage. But don't be afraid to let them try something new. When our kids were in this age range I spent many hours of time hauling them around to piano lessons, art classes, gymnastics, karate classes, and dance lessons, as well as museums of all sorts and live theater performances. They let me know whether they enjoyed this or that discipline. I could tell if they had a natural propensity toward something in particular. I listened to their reasons behind their dislikes and didn't push them too much further. This was their life. Why push them into something I wanted them to do? They got a rounded education in extracurricular activities, art, science and culture, and we all moved on. Goals should provide opportunities for growth, self-discovery, and the development of essential life skills, setting a foundation for success in adolescence and beyond.

Early Adolescence (Ages 12-14): As children enter adolescence, they experience significant intellectual and emotional development. Setting personal goals becomes instrumental in helping them navigate this period of change and self-discovery. Encouraging them to set goals related to time management, organization, and personal growth can enhance their self-esteem and resilience. Goal setting also aids in clarifying their values and aspirations, guiding them towards positive decision-making.

Grade Improvement: Encourage your child to set specific academic goals, such as achieving a certain GPA, earning higher grades in challenging subjects, or consistently completing assignments on time.

Study Skills: Help them develop effective study habits, including goal setting for daily or weekly study sessions and improving time management during homework and exam preparation.

Extracurricular Pursuits: Support their participation in extracurricular activities and set goals for achieving leadership roles or making significant contributions to clubs, teams, or organizations.

Time Management: Assist your child in refining their time management skills, setting schedules for school, extracurricular activities, and personal commitments.

Financial Literacy: Introduce basic concepts of money management, such as budgeting, saving, and understanding financial responsibility.

Organization: Encourage them to maintain an organized school binder, digital calendar, or planner to keep track of assignments, deadlines, and responsibilities.

Peer Relationships: Help them navigate peer relationships and set goals for developing and maintaining positive friendships, practicing empathy, and resolving conflicts constructively.

Communication Skills: Promote effective communication by setting goals for expressing thoughts and feelings clearly, actively listening, and advocating for themselves when necessary.

Resilience: Encourage the development of resilience by setting goals related to coping with stress, adversity, or setbacks in a healthy and constructive manner.

Healthy Lifestyle: Set goals for maintaining a balanced and healthy lifestyle, including regular physical activity, a nutritious diet, and adequate sleep.

Hygiene and Self-Care: Encourage personal hygiene and self-care routines, such as maintaining a skincare routine, practicing good oral hygiene, and developing healthy habits.

Mental Health Awareness: Promote awareness of mental health and well-being, setting goals for self-care practices like mindfulness, relaxation techniques, or seeking support when needed.

Career Exploration: Support their exploration of career interests and set goals for researching potential careers, seeking internships or job shadowing opportunities, or developing skills related to future career paths.

Hobbies and Interests: Encourage them to pursue hobbies and interests they are passionate about, setting goals for skill development or creating personal projects.

Community Involvement: Foster a sense of responsibility toward the community by encouraging volunteer work or involvement in service projects, setting goals for meaningful contributions.

These goals should be discussed collaboratively with your child to align with their interests and aspirations. They offer opportunities for personal growth, skill development, and the cultivation of responsible, well-rounded adolescents ready to face the challenges of the teenage years and beyond.

Late Adolescence (Ages 15-18): During the late adolescent years, setting goals becomes even more critical. As teenagers prepare for college or enter the workforce, encouraging them to set educational and career goals helps them define their path and take ownership of their future. This stage is also an excellent time to introduce longer-term goals, such as financial planning, leadership development, and building healthy relationships. Goal setting supports their transition into adulthood by promoting independence and self-determination.

College or Career Preparation: Assist your teenager in setting goals related to college applications, scholarship opportunities, or career exploration. Help them create a plan for standardized tests (e.g., SAT or ACT) and college essays.

Academic Excellence: Encourage setting goals for academic achievement, such as maintaining a high GPA, excelling in advanced courses, or pursuing academic honors.

Independent Research: Support them in undertaking independent research or projects related to their academic interests, which can strengthen their knowledge and skills in a particular field.

Financial Responsibility: Help your teenager set financial goals, such as budgeting, saving money, and understanding basic financial concepts like credit and taxes.

Driving and Transportation: If applicable, guide them through obtaining a driver's license and setting goals for responsible and safe driving practices.

Cooking and Nutrition: Encourage the development of culinary skills by setting goals for cooking meals, meal planning, and making nutritious food choices.

Physical Fitness: Support regular physical activity and fitness goals, whether it's participating in a sport, setting exercise routines, or working towards specific fitness achievements.

Mental Health Awareness: Promote mental health awareness and self-care practices, such as setting goals for stress management, seeking therapy or counseling when needed, and practicing mindfulness.

Healthy Lifestyle Choices: Guide them in making informed choices about substance use, including setting goals for avoiding harmful behaviors like smoking, alcohol, or drug misuse.

Internships and Job Experience: Encourage participation in internships, part-time jobs, or volunteer work to gain practical experience and set career-related goals.

Networking and Professional Development: Support them in building a network, attending conferences, or pursuing opportunities for professional growth in their chosen field.

Goal-Setting Workshops: Explore goal-setting workshops or resources that can help them refine their long-term career goals and personal development plans.

Leadership and Advocacy: Encourage your teenager to take on leadership roles in school clubs, community organizations, or advocacy groups, setting goals for their contributions and initiatives.

Volunteer and Service Goals: Foster a sense of responsibility toward the community by setting goals for volunteer work and service projects that align with their interests and passions.

Civic Engagement: Encourage participation in civic activities, such as voting, community meetings, or local initiatives, and set goals for active civic involvement.

You should discuss these goals with your teenager, considering their interests, aspirations, and developmental stage. They provide opportunities for personal growth, skill development, and the transition into adulthood, equipping them with the tools and experiences needed to navigate the challenges and opportunities of this stage of life.

Personal Responsibility: Setting personal goals instills a sense of responsibility in children and adolescents. When they set their own objectives, they take ownership of their actions and decisions. This fosters accountability, as they understand that they are responsible for the outcomes, whether positive or negative. Learning to set and achieve goals is a vital component of becoming a responsible and self-sufficient individual. Here are five examples of how kids can set their own personal goals and objectives:

Subject Improvement: Kids can set goals to improve their performance on a particular subject. For example, they might aim to raise their math grade from a B to an A by the end of the semester.

Reading Challenge: Encourage them to set a goal to read a certain number of books within a given time frame. This can help foster a love for reading while setting a clear and reachable target.

Physical Fitness: Children can set fitness goals like running a certain distance in a specific time or improving their strength and flexibility.

Healthy Eating: They can establish goals related to their diet, such as eating a serving of vegetables with every meal or reducing the consumption of sugary snacks.

Skill Acquisition: Kids can choose to learn a new skill or hobby, such as playing a musical instrument, painting, or coding, and set goals for skill development and proficiency.

Emotional Awareness: Encourage them to set goals related to their emotional well-being, such as identifying and expressing their feelings more openly or practicing mindfulness and relaxation techniques.

Chores and Household Responsibilities: Children can take charge of specific household chores and set goals for completing them regularly, such as making their bed daily or doing laundry on a set schedule.

Time Management: They can set goals for managing their time effectively, including establishing routines for homework, study sessions, and extracurricular activities.

Building Friendships: Kids can set goals for making new friends, being more sociable, or strengthening existing friendships by organizing playdates or starting conversations with peers.

Conflict Resolution: Encourage them to establish goals for resolving conflicts constructively, such as using "I" statements to express their feelings or finding compromises with siblings or friends.

To help children set and achieve these goals effectively, parents and caregivers can provide support and guidance, discuss their progress regularly, and celebrate their accomplishments along the way. This process not only promotes personal growth but also instills essential skills for self-motivation, planning, and perseverance.

Goal setting provides motivation and encourages persistence. When children have an obvious target, they are more likely to stay focused, work diligently, and persevere through challenges. Achieving their goals boosts their self-confidence and reinforces the idea that effort leads to success. This motivation extends beyond academics and can apply to extracurricular activities, hobbies, and personal growth, enriching various aspects of their lives.

Encouraging children to set personal goals at different stages of childhood and adolescence is essential for their development. It cultivates responsibility, motivation, and persistence, helping them build confidence, clarify their values, and take charge of their futures.

Parents, caregivers, and educators play a crucial role in guiding children through the goal-setting process, providing support and encouragement as they work towards their aspirations and dreams. Encouraging children to set personal goals is valuable because it promotes responsibility, independence, self-confidence, motivation, persistence, planning skills, self-reflection, and a sense of control over their own lives. These benefits contribute to their overall personal and academic development, preparing them to face life's challenges with confidence and resilience.

Handling Money: Teach them about money management. Give them an allowance and let them decide how to spend or save it. This helps them learn about budgeting and making choices with consequences. Teaching children and teenagers how to handle money responsibly is a valuable life skill that sets the foundation for financial well-being in adulthood. Here are five detailed examples of how to impart financial responsibility:

1. **Budgeting and Saving**

   Allowance Management: For younger children, provide a regular allowance and guide them to budget their money for various purposes, such as saving, spending, and sharing. Encourage them to set goals for saving towards specific items or experiences.

   Goal-Oriented Saving: For teenagers, introduce the concept of setting financial goals, like saving for a smartphone or a car. Help them create a budget that allocates a portion of their earnings or allowance toward these goals. Track their progress together and celebrate milestones.

2. **Understanding Needs vs. Wants**

   Discussion and Decision-Making: Engage children and teens in conversations about distinguishing between needs (essential items like food and clothing) and wants (desirable but non-essential items like video games or designer clothing). Encourage them to make thoughtful spending decisions based on this understanding.

3. **Earning and Work Ethic**

   Part-Time Jobs: For teenagers, encourage part-time employment or freelance opportunities, which provide a source of income and teach the value of hard work. Emphasize the importance of punctuality, responsibility, and professionalism in the workplace.

   Entrepreneurship: Encourage entrepreneurial endeavors, such as starting a small business or offering services like babysitting, lawn care, or tutoring. This fosters independence and business acumen.

4. **Banking and Financial Literacy**

   Opening a Bank Account: Help your child open a savings account at a local bank or credit union. Teach them how to make deposits, track transactions, and read bank statements. Discuss the concept of interest and how it can help their savings grow.

Financial Education: Introduce financial literacy by discussing concepts like credit, debt, interest rates, and investing. Encourage them to read books, take online courses, or attend workshops on personal finance.

5. **Smart Spending Habits**

   Comparative Shopping: Teach children and teens to compare prices and look for discounts or deals before making purchases. Emphasize the importance of avoiding impulsive buying and considering value for money.

   Delayed Gratification: Encourage them to practice delayed gratification by waiting before making significant purchases. Discuss the concept of saving up for a more substantial item rather than buying on credit.

   Throughout these lessons, parents and caregivers should lead by example, demonstrating responsible financial behavior and involving children and teens in real-life financial decisions when appropriate. The goal is to empower them with the knowledge and skills to make informed financial choices, avoid debt, and build a strong financial foundation for their future.

   Personal Care Choices: Allow them to make decisions about their personal care. For example, they can choose their own hairstyles, clothing styles, or even decide on a bedtime routine that works for them. Empowering children to make decisions about their own personal care is a crucial step in promoting their independence and building their self-confidence. Here are five detailed examples of how adults can allow children to make decisions in this area:

6. **Clothing Choices**

   Offer a Selection: Instead of laying out their outfits for them, provide children with a selection of clothing options that are appropriate for the weather and the occasion. Allow them to choose what they want to wear, promoting their autonomy and self-expression.

   Discuss Weather and Occasion: Engage in conversations about weather-appropriate clothing and dress codes for specific events, helping them understand the importance of dressing suitably for different situations.

7. **Meal Planning and Food Choices**

   Meal Participation: Involve children in meal planning and preparation. Allow them to have a say in selecting recipes, grocery shopping, and preparing meals, considering their dietary preferences and nutritional needs.

   Healthy Options: Educate them about the importance of a balanced diet and provide guidance on making healthy food choices. Encourage them to make informed decisions about snacks and meals.

8. **Personal Hygiene and Grooming**

   Choice of Toiletries: When it comes to personal care products like soap, shampoo, or toothpaste, let children choose their preferred scents or brands. This can make daily routines more enjoyable and help them take ownership of their personal hygiene.

   Establishing Routines: Work together to establish routines for brushing teeth, taking baths or showers, and other self-care activities. Allow them to decide the order in which they complete these tasks, giving them a sense of control.

9. **Bedtime and Sleep Routine**

   Setting Bedtime: Collaborate with children to set a reasonable bedtime that aligns with their age and school schedule. Let them be involved in the process of winding down and getting ready for bed.

   Bedtime Choices: Allow them to make choices about their bedtime routine, such as selecting a bedtime story, picking out pajamas, or deciding on a comforting nighttime ritual.

10. **Personal Space and Organization**

    Room Decor: Encourage children to personalize their living spaces, such as their bedroom or playroom. Let them choose decor items, posters, or colors that reflect their personality and style.

    Organization Strategies: Collaborate on organizing their belongings but let them have a say in how they arrange their space. This can include choosing storage solutions or deciding where specific items should go.

Throughout these processes, adults should provide guidance and boundaries while allowing room for age-appropriate decision-making. It's important to create a supportive and nurturing environment where children can learn to make choices, understand consequences, and gradually take on more responsibility for their personal care.

Encouraging independence in strong-willed children requires a delicate balance between guiding them and giving them the space to explore. Empowering them to embrace their independence is a journey that demands a delicate dance between guidance and freedom. In allowing them the space to explore, we provide them with opportunities to cultivate vital life skills and unlock their inner potential.

These experiences are not just steppingstones; they are the very foundation upon which they will build their futures. As they navigate the challenges and triumphs of self-reliance, each victory becomes a testament to their resilience and determination. With each obstacle they conquer, they forge a stronger sense of accomplishment that will not only serve them today but will light the path towards their successful journey into adulthood.

Parents play a pivotal role in their children's lives by imparting essential life skills, offering unwavering encouragement, and providing steadfast support throughout their formative years. This guidance not only equips children with the tools they need to navigate life's challenges, but also fosters a deep and meaningful bond between parents and their offspring. This strong connection remains intact until the day their children are prepared to spread their wings and leave the familial nest.

By nurturing this relationship and empowering their children to become self-sufficient, parents often experience a smoother transition when their kids eventually embark on their own journeys. The emptiness that can accompany an empty nest is mitigated, and parents can take solace in knowing that they have prepared their children for the world ahead, creating a foundation for a lifelong connection based on mutual respect and love.

CHAPTER 6

NEGOTIATE

Negotiating with strong-willed children holds significant importance in their development, as it equips them with valuable communication, problem-solving, and conflict resolution skills that are essential for navigating the complexities of the adult world. These spirited individuals possess a natural inclination to assert their preferences and opinions and teaching them how to negotiate effectively empowers them to express themselves while also understanding the importance of compromise and collaboration.

At its core, negotiation with strong-willed children helps them strike a balance between their assertiveness and adaptability. Encouraging them to voice their thoughts and desires while also guiding them to consider alternative perspectives instills a sense of empathy and openness to differing viewpoints. This ability to empathize and engage in meaningful conversations will prove invaluable as they interact with peers, colleagues, and authority figures throughout their lives.

Imagine a scenario where a child, let's call him Alex, wants to play his favorite board game with his friends at a sleepover. Alex is known for being assertive and really enjoys this game. However, his friends have other ideas and want to play a different game that not everyone knows how to play. In this situation, negotiation can help Alex reach a balance between his assertiveness and adaptability.

Instead of insisting on his choice and potentially causing conflict, Alex negotiates. He expresses his enthusiasm for playing the board game he loves, but also acknowledges his friends' desire to try something new. Alex suggests a compromise: they agree to play the new game first, giving it a fair chance, and afterward, everyone can play the board game Alex originally wanted.

Through this negotiation, Alex shows assertiveness by expressing his preference and adaptability by being open to trying something different. This approach fosters a harmonious atmosphere at the sleepover, allowing everyone to have a say and find a middle ground that satisfies everyone's desires. In the end, both assertiveness and adaptability play a role in making the evening enjoyable for all.

Negotiation fosters the development of critical thinking skills. Strong-willed children often possess a natural curiosity and a propensity to question the status quo. By engaging them in negotiation processes, parents stimulate their analytical thinking and encourage them to evaluate the merits and consequences of various options. This skill set enables them to make informed decisions and weigh the pros and cons of different choices, both in personal matters and in more complex situations they'll encounter as adults.

Let's consider a scenario where a child named Lily wants to decide how to spend her summer vacation. She has two main options: attending a summer camp or taking a family trip. In this situation, negotiation can stimulate Lily's analytical thinking and encourage her to evaluate the merits and consequences of these options.

Lily starts by discussing her preferences and concerns with her parents. She expresses her desire to go to summer camp, where she can make new friends and explore her interests in art and sports. On the other hand, she also values spending quality time with her family during a vacation.

Her parents recognize the importance of both options and decide to involve Lily in the decision-making process. They ask Lily to create a list of pros and cons for each choice. This exercise encourages her analytical thinking as she considers factors like personal growth, social interactions, and family bonding.

As Lily evaluates the merits and consequences of each option, she realizes that attending summer camp could provide unique learning opportunities and foster independence. However, she also understands that a family trip would create cherished memories and strengthen her bond with her parents and siblings.

Through negotiation and thoughtful analysis, Lily and her family eventually reach a decision that balances her desire for independence and her appreciation for family time. This experience not only helps her develop analytical thinking skills but also teaches her the value of making informed decisions based on careful consideration of the options and their consequences.

Negotiating also nurtures resilience. Through negotiation, strong-willed children learn that not every negotiation will result in getting everything they want. They experience the reality that sometimes compromises must be made, and setbacks are part of the process.

Consider a scenario where two siblings, Sarah and Mark, are negotiating the use of the family computer. Both have important tasks to complete. Sarah needs it for a school project due the next day, and Mark wants to play an online game with his friends. Their negotiation doesn't result in getting everything they want.

As they sit down to discuss the issue, they both express their needs and concerns. Sarah explains the urgency of her project and how it's essential for her grades. Mark talks about the game session he planned with his friends for weeks.

Despite their efforts to find a solution, it becomes clear that they can't both achieve their goals simultaneously. Sarah suggests they take turns with her using the computer for her project first, and Mark can have it afterward. This compromise means that neither of them gets exactly what they wanted at the exact time they wanted it.

Initially, both Sarah and Mark might feel disappointed or frustrated that they couldn't have everything their way. However, they come to understand that negotiations often involve making concessions and finding middle ground. They realize setbacks are part of the process, and sometimes, compromises are necessary to maintain peace and fairness within the family.

This scenario teaches them valuable life skills, such as conflict resolution, communication, and the importance of considering others' needs. It also emphasizes that in the real world, negotiations don't always result in getting everything you want, but finding common ground and making compromises can lead to mutually satisfactory outcomes. These experiences contribute to building emotional resilience and a willingness to adapt and learn from challenging situations.

In addition, the ability to negotiate empowers strong-willed children to advocate for themselves. They learn to articulate their needs, present their viewpoints, and work towards achieving their goals within the bounds of cooperation and respect.

Imagine a scenario where two friends, Mia and Ethan, are negotiating what game to play during their playdate. Mia wants to play her favorite board game, while Ethan prefers playing soccer outside. Negotiating in this situation can teach them to articulate their needs, present their viewpoints, and work towards achieving their goals within the bounds of cooperation and respect.

Mia starts by explaining how much she enjoys the board game and why it's essential for her to play it today. She says, "I really like this game, and it would make me happy to play it with you. We can have a lot of fun together."

Ethan, on the other hand, expresses his interest in soccer and shares his perspective. He says, "I love playing soccer, and it's a beautiful day outside. I think we could have a great time playing soccer together."

Recognizing that they have different preferences but wanting to maintain their friendship, Mia and Ethan decide to negotiate a compromise. They suggest they start by playing soccer outside for a while and then come inside to play the board game. This way, both of them get to enjoy their preferred activities during the playdate.

In this negotiation, Mia and Ethan learn to articulate their needs and viewpoints respectfully. They also discover the value of compromise and cooperation in maintaining their friendship while pursuing their individual interests. This scenario shows how negotiation can be a valuable skill for children, helping them navigate social interactions, build stronger relationships, and work towards shared solutions. This self-advocacy skill is a crucial aspect of self-confidence, ensuring they can stand up for themselves and assert their beliefs effectively.

In conclusion, negotiating with strong-willed children is a fundamental aspect of their personal growth and skill development. By imparting the art of negotiation, parents and caregivers equip these children with the tools they need to become effective communicators, critical thinkers, empathetic individuals, and resilient problem solvers. This ability to negotiate not only shapes their own success but also contributes positively to their interactions within their communities and the broader society.

Here are some quick examples of negotiating with strong-willed children:

Bedtime Negotiation: Child: "I don't want to go to bed at 8 PM. Can I stay up until 9 PM?" Parent: "I understand you'd like to stay up later. How about we compromise? On weekdays, you can stay up until 8:30 PM, and on weekends, we can extend it to 9 PM."

Homework Negotiation: Child: "I hate doing math homework. Can I do it after watching my favorite TV show?" Parent: "I know math can be challenging sometimes. How about we make a deal? You can do half of your math homework before the TV show and the other half afterward."

Screen Time Negotiation: Child: "I want to play video games for an hour." Parent: "I understand you enjoy playing games. Let's find a balance. You can have 30 minutes of game time now, and after that, let's spend 30 minutes together doing an activity you enjoy, like drawing or playing outside."

Chores Negotiation: Child: "I don't want to clean my room today." Parent: "I know cleaning your room isn't always fun. How about we work together to make it quicker? You pick up your toys, and I'll help you with the rest."

Mealtime Negotiation: Child: "I don't like broccoli. Can I have something else for dinner?" Parent: "I understand you don't like broccoli. How about we compromise? You can have a small portion of broccoli and also choose another vegetable you like to have on your plate."

Playtime Negotiation: Child: "I want to play outside, but my friends are coming over to play inside." Parent: "It sounds like you have a tough choice. How about you play inside with your friends for an hour and then spend an hour playing outside afterward?"

Clothing Negotiation: Child: "I don't want to wear this shirt. Can I wear my superhero shirt instead?" Parent: "I understand you have a favorite shirt. Today, we need to wear something a bit more formal, but you can wear your superhero shirt after we return home."

Playdate Negotiation: Child: "I want my friend to sleep over tonight." Parent: "Having a sleepover on a school night might be challenging. How about we plan for a sleepover on the weekend when we have more time? You can have your friend over for a playdate today instead."

These examples show how negotiation involves acknowledging the child's desires while finding middle ground or alternatives that work for both the child and the parent. Negotiating with strong-willed children helps them understand the concept of compromise and decision-making, promoting effective communication and collaboration skills.

CHAPTER 7

TESTING LIMITS

Strong-willed children exhibit assertive and determined personalities, often pushing their boundaries to the point of challenging their parents' patience. Dealing with strong-willed children who test limits repeatedly requires a delicate balance between patience and firmness. It's important to recognize that their behavior is often a manifestation of their innate desire to assert their independence and explore boundaries. Responding with a combination of patience and firmness can help establish clear expectations while nurturing their growth and development.

It's important to understand that a child's frustration or stubbornness moderates or balances their strong personalities in several ways. It can encourage them to slow down and think before acting impulsively, thereby teaching them patience and to consider alternative viewpoints or approaches. Dealing with frustration can increase empathy, as it forces individuals to understand the perspectives and feelings of others. This empathy can lead to more balanced interactions.

Stubbornness, when managed appropriately, can encourage flexibility and adaptability. It can push strong personalities to be open to compromise and new ideas. By recognizing the potential for conflict that their stubbornness may create, individuals may choose to moderate their behavior to maintain harmonious relationships.

While assertiveness and determination can characterize these powerful personalities, experiencing frustration or stubbornness can serve as a reminder to consider the feelings and needs of others, fostering more balanced and harmonious interactions.

A parent's patience is key when dealing with such situations. Strong-willed children are testing limits to understand their boundaries and to exert their autonomy. Responding with patience allows you to understand the underlying reasons behind their actions, fostering open communication and trust. Instead of reacting with frustration, take a deep breath and approach the situation calmly.

Imagine a scenario where a toddler named Leo is testing his limits by refusing to put on his shoes when it's time to leave for daycare. Instead of reacting with frustration, his parents respond with patience and empathy.

Leo starts by insisting, "I don't want to wear shoes!" His parents, recognizing that this is a common phase of asserting autonomy, take a patient approach. They crouch down to Leo's level, maintain a calm tone, and say, "I understand that you don't want to wear shoes right now. It's important to put on shoes so we can go to daycare. How about we choose your shoes together?"

Leo, still determined to assert his autonomy, may continue to resist. Instead of becoming frustrated, his parents continue to offer choices and empathy. They say, "I can see you want to decide. Would you like to wear the blue shoes or the red ones today?"

Leo, now feeling a sense of control and being heard, decides on the blue shoes. His parents help him put them on while engaging him in a conversation about his favorite color. Leo eventually cooperates, and they head off to daycare without a tantrum or power struggle.

In this example, Leo's parent responds to his testing of limits with patience, empathy, and an understanding that it's a natural part of a child's development. By offering choices and maintaining a calm demeanor, they help Leo assert his autonomy constructively, fostering a positive and cooperative environment. This approach not only diffuses potential frustration but also promotes a healthy parent-child relationship based on trust and respect.

The perception of inconsistency in rules or behavior can motivate strong-willed children to push boundaries further. Imagine a scenario where a child named Emily is testing boundaries related to screen time. Her parents have set clear limits of one hour of screen time per day during the school week. However, sometimes they allowed her to watch TV or play video games for longer periods on some days. Emily notices this inconsistency and sees it as a loophole to push against boundaries further.

One evening, Emily's parents are busy with chores, and they allow her to watch TV for an extended period without specifying a time limit. The next day, when they try to enforce the one-hour screen time rule, Emily protests, saying, "But yesterday, I got to watch TV for as long as I wanted!"

Emily's parents realize their inconsistency has created confusion and frustration for her. They acknowledge their mistake and explain that sometimes they may have made exceptions but that the general rule still applies. They emphasize the importance of maintaining consistency in rules and boundaries to ensure fairness and clarity.

Emily's perception of inconsistency as a loophole to challenge boundaries highlights the importance of parents maintaining consistent rules and consequences. Inconsistencies can lead to confusion and resistance from children, as they may exploit perceived loopholes in the rules. It's crucial for parents to communicate openly, admit when they make mistakes, and consistently reinforce established boundaries to create a stable and fair environment for their child.

At times like this, firmness is essential to maintain consistency and discipline. Being firm in your responses communicates that there are non-negotiable limits in place by providing clear boundaries and expectations. When a caregiver or parent responds with firmness, it sends a consistent message to the child that certain rules or limits are not open for debate. This clarity helps children understand the importance of respecting those boundaries and instills a sense of structure and discipline in their lives.

Firmness doesn't equate to harshness or punishment. Rather, it implies that certain rules or boundaries are necessary for safety, well-being, or an orderly household, and these limits should be consistently maintained. This approach ultimately helps children develop a sense of responsibility and an understanding of the consequences that come with crossing non-negotiable limits. While it's important to be patient, make it clear that certain behaviors are unacceptable, emphasizing the importance of rules and respect.

Using a patient and firm approach also means setting consequences that are reasonable along with being consistent. When a strong-willed child tests limits, calmly explain the consequences of their actions, and if they persist, follow through with the predetermined consequences. This consistency helps them understand that their actions have predictable outcomes, which is a valuable lesson for their future decision-making.

Let's consider a scenario where a teenager named Maya consistently comes home past her curfew despite her parents' rules. Her parents want to set consequences that are both reasonable and consistent to address this behavior.

After discussing the issue with Maya, her parents establish a reasonable consequence: If Maya arrives home past her curfew, she will lose her phone privileges for the following day. This consequence is reasonable because it directly relates to the issue and is not overly punitive. It also serves as a reminder of the importance of punctuality and responsibility.

Consistency is key in this scenario. Maya's parents make it clear that this consequence will be applied each time she breaks the curfew rule, with no exceptions. They explain that it's essential for her to understand the importance of respecting household rules and that the consequence is a way to reinforce this understanding.

In the following weeks, Maya arrives home on time more consistently, knowing that there are reasonable and consistent consequences in place for her actions. This approach allows her parents to address the issue effectively while maintaining a fair and predictable disciplinary process.

Engaging them in conversations about their behavior can also be helpful. Explain why certain limits are in place, allowing them to understand the rationale behind rules. This not only shows respect for their intelligence but also encourages them to internalize the principles you're trying to instill.

Imagine a situation where a child named Alex has been acting out in school, displaying disruptive behavior in the classroom. Rather than immediately resorting to discipline, Alex's teacher takes the initiative to engage him in a conversation about his behavior.

The teacher asks Alex to stay after class one day and, in a calm and non-confrontational manner, starts the conversation by saying, "Alex, I've noticed that there have been some disruptions in the classroom lately. Can you tell me what's been going on and how you're feeling about it?"

Alex, feeling that his teacher genuinely cares about his perspective, begins to open up. He shares that he's been feeling frustrated because he finds some of the lessons too challenging, and he's been having difficulty concentrating.

The teacher actively listens to Alex, empathizing with his struggles and acknowledging his feelings. She says, "Thank you for sharing that, Alex. It's completely normal to feel frustrated when you're facing challenges. Let's work together to find ways to help you with those subjects and improve your experience in the classroom."

By engaging Alex in this conversation about his behavior, the teacher not only gains insight into the underlying issues but also builds a foundation of trust and understanding. This approach fosters a more supportive and collaborative environment where Alex feels heard and empowered to address his challenges constructively, rather than resorting to disruptive behavior.

Here's another one: Let's take the example of a teenager named Sarah who is questioning the household rule of no electronic devices at the dinner table. Her parents want to engage her in a conversation to help her understand the rationale behind this rule.

One evening, as the family gathers for dinner, Sarah brings up the issue, saying, "I don't get why we can't use our phones during dinner. It's not like we're watching TV or anything."

Her parents respond by initiating a calm and respectful conversation, "I understand your question, Sarah. The reason we have this rule is to promote quality family time and better communication during meals. When we use our phones at the table, it's distracting for everyone at the table and we miss out on the opportunity to connect with each other."

The parents go on to explain that by putting away electronic devices during dinner, they can focus on each other, have meaningful conversations, and create a positive family atmosphere. "This gives us a sense of togetherness and strengthens the family bond," her dad says. "It gives us a special time to share stories, laughter, and catch up with one another," adds her mom. Her father continues, "It gives us time to enjoy each other's company when we all have such busy lives. Taking a break from technology even for a short while can improve relationships and create special memories around meals."

Sarah, now understanding the rationale behind the rule, appreciates the importance of family bonding and agrees to follow it. This example illustrates how engaging in a conversation to explain the reasoning behind a rule can help children and teenagers comprehend the purpose behind it, fostering their cooperation and understanding.

Offering alternative ways for them to assert their independence within acceptable boundaries is another approach. If they want to challenge rules, provide opportunities for them to make choices and decisions that align with the rules. This empowers them while reinforcing the fact that there are still limits in place.

Last, remember that consistency, patience, and firmness go hand in hand. Being consistent in your approach reinforces the message that you're unwavering in your expectations, while patience allows them the time and space to understand and adapt to those expectations.

Through this balanced approach, you guide strong-willed children toward becoming responsible, self-aware, and respectful individuals who understand the importance of rules while still expressing their individuality.

Here are some more examples that illustrate the combination of patience and firmness when dealing with strong-willed children testing their limits repeatedly:

Bedtime Resistance: Child: "I don't want to go to bed now!" Parent (Firm): "I understand that you want to stay up, but it's bedtime. We need to stick to our routine. We can read a story before bed, but it's time to sleep."

Refusing to Do Homework: Child: "I don't want to do my homework. It's boring." Parent (Firm): "I know homework can be challenging, but it's part of our responsibilities. Let's start with math today. Once we finish that, you can take a short break."

Screen Time Negotiation: Child: "Just a few more minutes on the tablet, please!" Parent (Firm): "Our screen time limit is up for the day. We talked about this earlier. It's time to turn it off and find something else to do."

Mealtime Preferences: Child: "I won't eat these vegetables." Parent (Firm): "Vegetables are important for our health. You don't have to finish them all, but you need to try a few bites. If you're still hungry after dinner, we can have a healthy snack."

Toy Cleanup: Child: "I don't want to clean up my toys." Parent (Firm): "Cleaning up after playtime is part of taking care of our things. If you don't clean up, we might need to put the toys away for a while."

Getting Ready for School: Child: "I won't put on my shoes!" Parent (Firm): "Getting ready for school is important. We need to leave on time. You can put on your shoes now, or I'll help you put them on, but we have to get going."

Outdoor Play Safety: Child: "I don't need to wear my helmet!" Parent (Firm): "Safety is important. When we ride bikes, we always wear helmets. It's a rule to protect ourselves. If you don't want to wear a helmet, we won't be able to ride today."

Respecting Personal Space: Child: "I want to play with your phone!" Parent (Firm): "I understand you're curious, but my phone is not a toy. We have rules about using it. You can play with your toys instead."

In each of these examples, the parent responds with firmness by setting clear expectations, explaining rules, and stating consequences when necessary. However, they also exhibit patience by acknowledging the child's feelings, explaining reasons behind the rules, and allowing space for the child to express themselves. This balanced approach helps the strong-willed child understand the boundaries while feeling heard and understood.

CHAPTER 8

POSITIVE REINFORCEMENT

Providing positive reinforcement to your strong-willed child is a powerful approach that can significantly affect their behavior, self-esteem, and overall development. These determined individuals often respond well to praise and encouragement, making positive reinforcement an effective tool for guiding them toward positive choices and actions.

First, positive reinforcement creates a supportive and nurturing environment. Positive reinforcement fosters positive interactions and enhances relationships. When parents, caregivers, teachers, or peers acknowledge and praise one another for their efforts and accomplishments, it creates a sense of connection and trust—it strengthens relationships. In such an environment, individuals feel safe, respected, and valued. By acknowledging their efforts and successes, you convey that you value and appreciate their unique qualities. This gives a sense of belonging and connection, helping to build a strong parent-child relationship based on trust and mutual respect.

Positive reinforcement reinforces desired behavior. Positive reinforcement involves acknowledging and rewarding desired behaviors. When individuals, especially children, experience praise, rewards, or affirmation for their positive actions, they are more likely to repeat those behaviors. By focusing on the positive and rewarding desired behaviors, positive reinforcement can help reduce negative behavior.

Consistently recognizing and rewarding individuals for their efforts to make constructive choices reduces their inclination to engage in disruptive or harmful behaviors. This sets a foundation for a harmonious and cooperative atmosphere. This is particularly important for strong-willed children, as it helps them understand which behaviors align with your expectations and family values.

Positive reinforcement also boosts their self-esteem and confidence. Regularly recognizing their achievements and efforts boosts their self-image and encourages them to view themselves as capable individuals. When people receive positive reinforcement, they feel valued and appreciated. This boost in self-esteem can lead to increased confidence and a greater sense of self-worth. A nurturing environment promotes individuals to take healthy risks, try new things, and believe in themselves. All this rolls over into the mind of the child and encourages intrinsic motivation. Instead of relying solely on external rewards, it helps strong-willed children develop a sense of pride and satisfaction from their accomplishments. This intrinsic motivation drives them to make positive choices, even when immediate rewards are not present.

Positive reinforcement provides an alternative to negative attention-seeking behaviors. If strong-willed children feel that they only receive attention when they're misbehaving, they may continue negative behaviors to garner attention. Offering praise for positive behaviors shows them they can receive attention and validation through constructive actions, not destructive actions.

Using money as a form of positive reinforcement can be effective in teaching financial responsibility and work ethics. For example, parents may choose to give their children an allowance for completing household chores or achieving academic goals. This not only motivates children to contribute to the family's well-being but also helps them learn the value of money, budgeting, and saving.

In the workplace, monetary incentives such as bonuses, commissions, or raises can serve as powerful positive reinforcement tools. These financial rewards can motivate employees to meet or exceed performance targets, fostering a culture of productivity and excellence. However, it's crucial for employers to ensure that these incentives are fair, transparent, and aligned with the organization's values and goals. The same goes for children of all ages. As they age, their inclination towards pricier toys and gadgets grows, driving them to desire higher earnings and motivating them to work harder for larger bonuses.

I used to offer my children a monetary incentive for every A on their report cards. Initially, they didn't show much enthusiasm, but as they matured and their unique personalities emerged, they started aiming for higher grades, motivated by the desire to save for specific items. One daughter diligently saved up for a new saddle, while her sister set her sights on acquiring a fresh wardrobe. Meanwhile, one of our sons earmarked his savings for electronic and computer components, while the younger one had his eyes on games for his Gameboy. Their dedication to academic excellence, marked by consistent A's on their report cards, became a habit that persisted even after the monetary incentives were no longer in place.

Remember, offering money as positive reinforcement should be balanced with non-monetary rewards like praise, recognition, and opportunities for personal growth. Overemphasizing monetary rewards might lead to a shallow focus on financial gain rather than intrinsic motivation or passion for the task at hand. A well-rounded approach that combines financial incentives with non-monetary forms of positive reinforcement can create a more holistic and motivating environment for individuals to thrive.

In conclusion, giving positive reinforcement to strong-willed children is a valuable strategy for shaping their behavior, building their self-esteem, and nurturing their growth. By creating an environment of support, promoting desired behavior, boosting their self-confidence, fostering intrinsic motivation, and redirecting attention-seeking tendencies, positive reinforcement equips these children with the tools they need to develop into well-adjusted, self-assured, and positively contributing individuals.

Here are some examples of giving positive reinforcement to your strong-willed child:

Chores and Responsibilities: Child: Successfully completes their assigned chores without reminders. Parent: "I'm really impressed with how responsible you've been with your chores. Your effort makes a big difference in keeping our home organized."

Homework Accomplishment: Child: Completes their homework on time and shows an improvement in their grades. Parent: "I noticed you've been putting in a lot of effort with your homework. Your hard work is paying off, and I'm proud of your progress."

Sharing and Cooperation: Child: Shares a toy with a sibling or friend without being prompted. Parent: "I saw how nicely you shared your toy with your sister. That's a kind and thoughtful thing to do."

Emotional Regulation: Child: Handles a frustrating situation without losing their temper. Parent: "I know that situation was tough, but I'm really proud of how you kept your cool and handled it calmly."

Decision-Making: Child: Makes a responsible decision independently, like choosing a healthy snack over junk food. Parent: "I noticed you made a superb choice by picking a healthy snack. It's important to take care of our bodies, and you're making smart decisions."

Communication Skills: Child: Expresses their thoughts and feelings openly and respectfully during a conversation. Parent: "I appreciate how well you communicate your ideas. It shows maturity and consideration for others."

Creative Achievements: Child: Creates a piece of art, story, or project. Parent: "Your creativity really shines through in your artwork. You put a lot of thought and effort into your projects, and it shows."

Helping Others: Child: Offers assistance to someone, like helping a family member with a task. Parent: "Your willingness to help others is wonderful. Your kindness doesn't go unnoticed, and it makes a positive impact on those around you."

Problem-Solving: Child: Comes up with a solution to a challenge they're facing. Parent: "I'm proud of your problem-solving skills. Finding solutions to challenges is a valuable skill that will serve you well in life."

In each of these examples, positive reinforcement involves a specific acknowledgment of the child's actions and efforts. It highlights their strengths, encourages positive behavior, and reinforces their self-esteem and confidence. This positive feedback fosters a sense of accomplishment and motivates them to continue making constructive choices and contributions.

CHAPTER 9

MODEL BEHAVIOR

Modeling behavior in front of your strong-willed children is a powerful way to shape their attitudes, values, and actions. These children are keen observers, and they learn by example. Therefore, being a positive role model holds immense significance in their development.

Children naturally imitate the behaviors they see around them, particularly those exhibited by their parents or caregivers. By consistently showing respectful communication, empathy, responsibility, and other positive traits, you provide a blueprint for how they should interact with others and handle different situations.

Modeling behavior teaches them valuable life skills. When they witness you managing stress, problem-solving, and making responsible choices, they learn how to navigate challenges effectively. These skills become a foundation for their own decision-making as they grow and face increasingly complex situations.

When children see adults effectively managing stress, they learn valuable lessons about emotional regulation, resilience, and healthy coping mechanisms. By observing how adults handle challenging situations, kids can internalize these essential life skills. They learn that stress is a normal part of life and that it's possible to navigate it in constructive ways. First, children pick up on the importance of staying calm under pressure. When adults model composed and rational responses to stressors, children learn how to keep their emotions in check and think more clearly when faced with difficulties.

Second, kids witness problem-solving skills in action. Adults who manage stress effectively often engage in problem-solving rather than reacting impulsively. Children learn to approach challenges methodically, seek solutions, and adapt to changing circumstances. This applies even if these lessons from you, as the parent and primary caregiver, are skewed, or there is abuse that they watch on a daily basis (whether mental or physical). These children will imitate *you* in their own lives. Their adult lives will also be skewed, or they may take or dish out abuse because they grew up believing that these are normal behaviors in relationships.

Children learn the significance of self-care and stress reduction techniques by watching you. Adults who prioritize self-care activities like exercise, mindfulness, or seeking support through social connections teach children the importance of taking care of their mental and emotional well-being.

On the other hand, children who watch a parent drink alcohol as a means of stress-relief learn that this is an acceptable means of self-care. Children absorb all these critical lessons about emotional regulation, problem-solving, and self-care from watching *you* from the time they are born. These lessons equip them with the skills and resilience needed to navigate life's inevitable challenges in a healthy and constructive manner—or not.

Demonstrating empathetic and compassionate behavior serves as a potent method for nurturing these qualities in children. When children observe adults consistently showing empathy and kindness toward others, they internalize these behaviors as social norms and are more likely to replicate them in their own interactions. By witnessing acts of kindness and understanding, children learn that it's essential to consider others' feelings, needs, and perspectives.

Modeling also offers children practical, real-life examples of how to express empathy and kindness in a wide range of situations. When adults exhibit these behaviors, whether by helping a neighbor in need, offering support to a friend, or showing compassion to someone facing difficulties, children witness the positive impact such actions can have on others. This firsthand experience encourages them to engage in similar acts of kindness and empathy. When you show empathy toward others and engage in acts of kindness, you set an example for them to follow. This paves the way for them to become compassionate individuals who care about the well-being of others and contribute positively to their communities.

When adults model empathy and kindness, they create a nurturing and emotionally safe environment where children feel both valued and understood. This encourages children to develop their own emotional intelligence, allowing them to connect with others on a deeper level and foster positive relationships based on empathy, kindness, and mutual respect. Modeling serves as a foundational tool in shaping children's character and values, emphasizing the significance of empathy and kindness in creating a compassionate and harmonious society.

Modeling behavior also offers a consistent framework for understanding and internalizing core values, such as honesty, integrity, respect, and perseverance. When children see adults consistently embodying these values in their actions and interactions, it provides them with clear and tangible examples to follow. For instance, when adults consistently tell the truth, honor their commitments, show respect to others, and persist in the face of challenges, children learn that these values are not just abstract concepts but practical principles to live by.

Consistent modeling also shows that these values are not situational. Children observe that honesty isn't just about not telling lies but also being truthful in all their interactions, and that respect isn't limited to certain people or situations but extends to everyone. This consistency helps children develop a deep understanding of the importance of these values in guiding their behavior and decision-making.

Modeling provides children with a moral compass, helping them navigate the complexities of the world by providing concrete examples of how to apply these values in different contexts. As children witness adults embodying these principles, they are more likely to internalize them, leading to the development of strong moral and ethical foundations that will shape their actions and choices throughout their lives. Modeling behavior creates a living, breathing framework for understanding and embracing values that contribute to ethical, responsible, and principled individuals.

Modeling behavior plays a significant role in encouraging a growth mindset both in children and adults. When individuals consistently show a growth mindset in their actions, they show that they believe in the power of effort, learning, and resilience. When individuals consistently model a growth mindset in their actions, they communicate their belief in the power of effort, learning, and resilience, and that intelligence and abilities can be developed through dedication and perseverance.

When children see adults embracing challenges, seeking opportunities for growth, and persisting through setbacks, they internalize the idea that setbacks and failures are not indicators of inadequacy but rather steppingstones to improvement. This modeling shows that making mistakes is a natural part of the learning process and that effort is a crucial component of success.

Adults who model a growth mindset provide inspiration and motivation for those around them. When individuals observe that their parents, teachers, or mentors are continuously learning, adapting, and striving for self-improvement, they are more likely to follow suit. This creates a culture of curiosity, resilience, and a belief in one's ability to develop and grow.

In summary, modeling a growth mindset through consistent behavior fosters a mindset shift in others by demonstrating the power of effort and a willingness to learn from experiences. It encourages individuals to embrace challenges, persist through difficulties, and ultimately realize their potential for growth and development in various aspects of life.

Modeling behavior is a powerful tool for promoting healthy emotional expression and teaching constructive ways to manage emotions. When adults consistently show emotionally intelligent behavior, such as expressing their feelings openly and managing them in a healthy manner, children, and others around them learn essential skills for emotional well-being. By observing adults who communicate their emotions calmly and assertively, children learn that it's okay to feel and express their feelings without fear of judgment or criticism. This modeling encourages an environment where emotional expression is valued and respected.

Adults who model constructive ways to manage emotions, such as deep breathing exercises, mindfulness techniques, or seeking support when needed, teach valuable coping strategies. Children witnessing these behaviors recognize that managing emotions is not about suppressing or avoiding them, but about dealing with them effectively and healthily.

Consistent modeling also emphasizes the importance of empathy and understanding in interpersonal relationships. When adults acknowledge and validate others' emotions, they teach individuals how to create a supportive and empathetic environment where emotions are addressed constructively.

Modeling behavior fosters healthy emotional expression and equips children with the tools to manage their emotions constructively. Modeling behavior creates a culture of emotional intelligence, where we acknowledge, express, and manage feelings in ways that promote well-being and positive relationships. When you openly share your emotions and show constructive ways to manage them, you teach your children that emotions are natural and can be dealt with in healthy ways. This encourages emotional intelligence and well-being in your children.

Modeling behavior also serves as the cornerstone for effective communication with children. When adults consistently exhibit positive communication patterns, they create a nurturing environment that encourages open and honest dialogue. Children observe and internalize these patterns, shaping their own communication skills and fostering a firm foundation for meaningful interactions.

Regarding effective communication, modeling active listening is crucial. When adults actively listen to their children by giving them their full attention, making eye contact, and empathizing with their feelings and concerns, it teaches children the importance of being heard and valued. As a result, children are more inclined to imitate this active listening behavior, leading to increased empathy and understanding in their interactions.

Second, modeling respect and courtesy in communication is key. When adults consistently show respect by using polite language, maintaining a calm tone, and avoiding disrespectful or offensive speech, children learn how to engage in respectful conversations. Children understand that effective communication is not about dominating the conversation but about creating a space where everyone's voice is valued.

Adults who model conflict resolution techniques, such as compromising, seeking common ground, and managing disagreements calmly, provide children with valuable tools for handling conflicts in their own lives. Children observe how dialogue and compromise can resolve conflicts instead of aggression or avoidance.

It is important to model emotional expression and vulnerability in order to create a safe space for children to share their thoughts and feelings. When adults openly express their own emotions and discuss them in a healthy and constructive manner, children also learn to articulate their feelings and concerns effectively, leading to more honest and meaningful conversations.

In summary, modeling behavior lays the groundwork for effective communication with children by teaching them active listening, respect, conflict resolution, and emotional expression. By consistently applying these communication skills in their own lives, adults create an environment where children feel valued, heard, and empowered to engage in open and constructive dialogue. When your children witness you actively listening, expressing yourself clearly, and resolving conflicts peacefully, they learn how to communicate effectively and build positive relationships.

Modeling behavior plays a pivotal role in nurturing a strong and healthy parent-child relationship. When parents consistently model positive behavior, they set the tone for the dynamics within the relationship and create a foundation built on trust, respect, and mutual understanding. For example, when parents consistently model empathy and understanding, they show children they value and acknowledge their feelings and perspectives. When parents actively listen, empathize with their children's emotions, and respond with patience and compassion, it fosters a sense of emotional connection and safety within the relationship.

Modeling open and effective communication sets the stage for honest and meaningful interactions. When parents communicate openly, respectfully, and transparently, it encourages their children to do the same. This creates an atmosphere where both parents and children feel comfortable discussing their thoughts, concerns, and feelings, strengthening the bond between them.

Modeling problem-solving and conflict resolution skills equips children with essential tools for navigating challenges and disagreements in a healthy way. When parents consistently handle conflicts calmly, seek compromise, and find common ground in their own lives, they show their children that disagreements are a natural part of relationships and can be resolved constructively.

Teaching values and principles through modeling behavior strengthens the parent-child relationship. When parents consistently exhibit qualities such as kindness, integrity, honesty, and perseverance, they provide their children with ethical and moral frameworks that shape their own behavior and choices. All of this nurtures a strong parent-child relationship. When your behaviors align with your words, they learn to trust and respect your guidance. This trust forms the basis for open communication and a healthy connection that supports their emotional and psychological growth. Most importantly, it leads to a deeper connection of mutual respect and a harmonious relationship built on love and understanding.

In summary, modeling behavior is essential for nurturing determined children who become balanced and accountable adults. Your actions speak louder than words, and by consistently embodying the traits and values you wish to instill in them, you provide a roadmap for their personal and ethical development.

Here are some examples of modeling behavior for your strong-willed child:

Respectful Communication: Model: When discussing differences of opinion with your partner, you maintain a calm tone and listen attentively. Impact: Your child learns that disagreements can be handled respectfully and without resorting to raised voices or hurtful language.

Empathy and Kindness: Model: You help a neighbor who is struggling with heavy bags of groceries, showing kindness and willingness to assist. Impact: Your child observes that being considerate and helping others in need is an important part of being a compassionate person.

Responsibility: Model: You consistently complete your work tasks on time and manage household responsibilities efficiently. Impact: Your child learns the importance of fulfilling responsibilities and managing time effectively.

Problem-Solving: Model: When facing a challenging situation, you openly discuss potential solutions and weigh their pros and cons. Impact: Seeing that challenges can be tackled methodically encourages your child to approach problems with a constructive mindset.

Growth Mindset: Model: You take up a new hobby or skill, showing enthusiasm for learning something new even if it involves initial struggles. Impact: Your child understands that growth comes from embracing challenges and that failures are steppingstones to improvement.

Emotional Expression: Model: You openly discuss your emotions when you're feeling happy, sad, or frustrated, and explain how you manage them. Impact: Your child learns that emotions are normal, and they gain insights into how to handle their own feelings in healthy ways.

Effective Communication: Model: You actively listen and engage in conversations with friends, showing respect for their opinions and asking questions to understand them better. Impact: Your child learns the importance of being a good listener and taking part in meaningful discussions.

Personal Growth: Model: You set personal goals for physical fitness and work consistently to achieve them. Impact: Your child witnesses the value of setting goals, committing to self-improvement, and working diligently to attain them.

Conflict Resolution: Model: You resolve disagreements with family members by calmly discussing the issues and finding compromises. Impact: Your child learns that conflicts can be resolved through open communication and negotiation, rather than resorting to arguments.

In each of these examples, your behavior serves as a direct example for your strong-willed child to observe and learn from. Modeling these positive behaviors helps them internalize important life skills, values, and attitudes that will shape their character and actions in the years to come.

CHAPTER 10

PROBLEM-SOLVING SKILLS

Equipping your strong-willed child with problem-solving skills is crucial for their personal growth and development, as it empowers them to tackle challenges, make wise choices, and face life confidently. Strong-willed children often possess an innate determination and curiosity, making them particularly receptive to learning problem-solving techniques that can harness these qualities effectively.

The fun part of helping your strong-willed child develop problem-solving skills is the opportunity for dynamic and engaging interactions that tap into their natural determination and curiosity. It can be enjoyable because strong-willed children often have a unique perspective and can think outside the box. When you engage them in problem-solving activities, you might be surprised by their creative and innovative ideas. It's fun to see their minds at work as they come up with solutions you might not have considered.

Another entertaining aspect is that strong-willed children tend to enjoy a good debate. Problem-solving discussions can turn into lively debates where you both get to share your viewpoints, learn from each other, and engage in intellectual challenges. It's an opportunity for healthy intellectual sparring that can be quite enjoyable.

Witnessing your strong-willed child successfully solve a problem can be incredibly satisfying. Their determination and persistence pay off, and it's rewarding for both you and them to see their efforts lead to a solution. This sense of accomplishment can boost their self-esteem and provide a shared sense of pride.

Problem-solving helps build resilience, and strong-willed children thrive on challenges. When they face difficulties head-on and work through them, it's gratifying to witness them pick themselves up, dust themselves off and keep on going. Their resilience is awesome to watch, especially as the challenges get harder as they get older. They understand setbacks are a part of life, and they develop the skills to bounce back from disappointments and failures, which is essential for their emotional well-being. It's a reminder to us (the parent, guardian, or caregiver) of their inner strength and ability to handle adversity.

Teaching problem-solving skills to strong-willed children is a valuable life lesson for both the child and the parent. It's enjoyable as well as reassuring to know that you're equipping them with essential skills they'll carry with them into adulthood, helping them navigate life's complexities effectively. Sometimes it is quite humorous to the parents as they literally observe their child's brain working by watching the expressions on his or her face change as the child begins to understand the importance of communication, compromise, and empathy in resolving disputes.

Collaborative problem-solving can also be a bonding experience. It fosters open communication, mutual respect, and a sense of teamwork. The shared effort to overcome challenges can strengthen the parent-child relationship. Moreover, it allows parents and children to better understand each other's perspectives and work together as a team, which ultimately deepens their connection. The shared journey of overcoming obstacles can be a powerful tool for fortifying the parent-child relationship.

Helping your strong-willed child with problem-solving skills can be fun because it taps into their innate determination and intelligence. It provides opportunities for engaging conversations, creative thinking, and shared successes, making the journey of parenting a strong-willed child even more rewarding.

Now, let's delve into the nuances of the advantages of problem-solving skills and the positive outcomes that arise from imparting them to your children. First, problem-solving skills empower children to tackle difficulties independently. By teaching them how to identify issues, analyze them critically, and plan solutions, you're enabling them to navigate challenges with resilience and self-reliance. This promotes a sense of empowerment, reducing their reliance on others to resolve problems.

By working with your children in problem solving, you are helping them build a toolkit of strategies and a sense of self-efficacy. As children develop these skills, they learn to approach challenges with confidence rather than fear. They become more self-reliant and less dependent on others for solutions, fostering a sense of autonomy and competence.

Problem-solving skills equip children with the ability to break down complex problems into manageable steps. This process of breaking a problem into smaller, more manageable parts enables them to approach challenges methodically, identifying potential solutions and evaluating each solution's effectiveness. They come to understand that setbacks and failures are part of the problem-solving process. They learn to persevere in the face of obstacles. This resilience not only helps them overcome immediate challenges but also builds emotional strength and adaptability, enabling them to navigate future difficulties with more confidence.

These skills encourage critical thinking and creativity. Problem-solving skills play a pivotal role in encouraging critical thinking in children. When children face challenges or puzzles, they learn to analyze the situation, identify potential solutions, and assess the pros and cons of each option. This process of critical thinking encourages them to question assumptions, consider alternative perspectives, and make informed decisions. Over time, as they apply problem-solving skills to various situations, they develop a deeper capacity for critical thinking, which becomes a valuable asset in academic pursuits, decision-making, and problem-solving in their daily lives.

Children learn how to analyze things through a combination of innate curiosity, exposure to new experiences, guidance from adults, and educational opportunities. From a very young age, children are keen observers of their surroundings. They naturally use their senses to take in information and notice patterns, differences, and similarities in the world around them. Play is a fundamental way for children to learn and practice analysis. Through imaginative play, building with blocks, or solving puzzles, they develop spatial reasoning and problem-solving abilities. Play also allows them to experiment, make hypotheses, and draw conclusions.

Parents, caregivers, and teachers play a crucial role in nurturing analytical skills. They can introduce children to new concepts, encourage critical thinking, and provide guidance on how to approach problems and find solutions. Children are naturally curious and often ask non-stop questions to better understand the world. Encouraging their inquiries and providing thoughtful answers fosters analytical thinking. Adults can also guide children to ask deeper and more complex questions as they grow.

Formal education, including school and extracurricular activities, offers structured opportunities for children to enhance their analytical abilities. Subjects like math, science, and reading encourage systematic analysis, logical reasoning, and problem-solving. Challenges force analytical thinking, whether it's completing a hard puzzle, resolving a conflict with a friend, or understanding a complex story. Children also model the analytical behavior they observe in adults. When they see parents or teachers using critical thinking and problem-solving skills in their daily lives, it encourages them to do the same.

Technology can play a significant role in promoting analytical thinking in kids when used in a thoughtful and educational manner. In today's digital age, children often interact with technology, through educational apps, games, and online resources, all of which offer engaging opportunities to solve problems and explore various subjects.

Technology allows children to interact with math and science concepts through simulations and virtual experiments. These tools encourage them to analyze data, make predictions, and draw conclusions based on their observations. There are apps specifically designed to stimulate problem-solving skills. These apps present various scenarios or puzzles that children must analyze and solve using logic and reasoning. Encouraging kids to create digital stories or multimedia presentations can foster analytical thinking. They need to plan, organize, and structure their narratives, making decisions about content, sequencing, and visuals.

Some software tools and apps help kids work with data, allowing them to input, manipulate, and analyze information. This can be particularly valuable in developing analytical skills related to statistics and data interpretation. Learning to code not only teaches computational thinking, but also promotes analytical skills. Kids can break down problems into smaller steps, identify patterns, and use logical reasoning to create programs or solve coding challenges.

Well-curated educational videos and documentaries can provide opportunities for kids to analyze information, make connections between concepts, and think critically about the content presented. Technology platforms often host educational challenges and competitions that require analytical thinking. These events can motivate kids to solve problems and think critically to achieve specific goals.

To make the most of technology for promoting analytical thinking in kids, parents and educators should ensure that they balance screen time with other activities and provide guidance and supervision as children use technology. Encouraging discussions about what they are learning and experiencing online can further enhance the analytical thinking process. It's essential to strike a balance between using technology as a tool for learning and maintaining a well-rounded educational experience that includes offline activities and social interactions.

There is no question that problem-solving skills promote critical thinking. Children learn how to analyze things through a combination of innate curiosity, experiential learning, guidance, and educational opportunities. These skills develop and evolve over time through practice and exposure to increasingly complex challenges. Encouraging strong-willed children to evaluate different options, weigh consequences, and consider various perspectives sharpens their analytical thinking. This mental agility not only helps them solve immediate problems but also fosters a mindset of curiosity and exploration. It is an asset that they can apply to future academic, professional, and personal endeavors.

Problem-solving skills and creativity are closely intertwined and fostering one can enhance the other. Strong-willed children often possess vivid imaginations and a willingness to explore unconventional approaches. Guiding them through problem-solving processes encourages them to think outside the box, leading to innovative solutions that others might not have considered.

Problem-solving skills foster and support creativity, like recognizing challenges and identifying opportunities in various situations. Problem solvers often employ divergent thinking, which is the ability to generate multiple ideas or solutions for a single problem. This creative thinking process encourages the exploration of unconventional and imaginative approaches.

Brainstorming and experimentation are inherently creative processes of problem solving. Creativity also involves connecting seemingly unrelated ideas or concepts to generate novel solutions or insights. Problem solvers excel at making these connections when seeking solutions to complex problems.

Problem solving fosters an open-minded attitude—a creative mind that is receptive to different viewpoints and ideas, especially in the face of uncertainty. Creative individuals are comfortable navigating these uncertainties and using them as a springboard for more creative exploration, sometimes drawing from various disciplines and fields through numerous trial-and-error processes.

Problem-solving skills provide a strong foundation for creativity by encouraging individuals to explore, experiment, and think critically when faced with challenges. The iterative nature of problem-solving, coupled with open-mindedness and a willingness to embrace ambiguity, can lead to the generation of novel and imaginative ideas. When problem-solving and creativity are nurtured together, individuals become better equipped to tackle complex issues in innovative ways, fostering a culture of continuous improvement and innovation in various aspects of life, including business, art, science, and everyday problem-solving scenarios.

Additionally, problem-solving skills instill adaptability. Life is unpredictable, and effective problem solvers are adaptable. They are better equipped to handle unexpected changes and adapt to new situations. This adaptability is a crucial asset in adulthood, where one often faces shifting circumstances and challenges. As they encounter varying situations and obstacles, these children learn to approach each scenario with a flexible mindset, adjusting their strategies as needed. This adaptability is an essential trait in a world that constantly presents new challenges and opportunities.

Older people who haven't received explicit teaching or exposure to adaptability skills during their formative years may face challenges in adapting to societal changes. I'm sure you know a few people who seem to be stuck in what I call a "time warp,"—people who just can't adjust to new ideas, technologies, or ways of doing things.

Because of their lack of cognitive flexibility, many elderly people struggle with change and experience emotional difficulty when trying to break out of established routines, habits, and comfort zones. The unknown is scary to them. They have smaller social circles because adapting to new social norms or making new connections can be daunting for them. Even adapting to changes that require physical activity for the benefit of their health is next to impossible for many elderly people who were not taught these problem-solving skills as children. Not to mention rapid technological advancements which can be particularly intimidating for older individuals who didn't grow up with these problem-solving tools.

Open your eyes. Look around. It is sad to see so many people facing these problems. You could find yourself observing your own parents grappling with the challenges of adapting to the evolving norms of each generation. It's possible to feel exasperated with your parents for not prioritizing their health, even if it means making the smallest effort to engage in physical activity. However, there are elderly individuals whose parents instilled in them a problem-solving toolkit, and these are the sixty, seventy, and eighty-year-olds you can spot in the gym, confidently holding a cellphone as they plan their next adventure online.

While writing this segment on the importance of how teaching children problem-solving skills promotes adaptability, I had an Ah-Ha Moment about my youth. I realized I wasn't taught anything about adaptability, creativity, critical thinking, or problem solving by my parents. My parents raised me in a rigid environment - they had Type A personalities and were both dogmatic perfectionists. "It is what it is because I said so." "Don't question anything I say, because what I say is the truth." "If it is written in this or that book (not referring to the Bible here) it has to be true." "Don't read fiction. It's a waste of time." You get the picture.

There was no room for me to grow, intellectually or creatively, or to develop analytical skills through problem solving. The school of hard knocks helped me develop problem-solving skills and flexibility. I drifted downstream on the river of life, embracing any easy tributaries that came my way. I didn't have the confidence to say, "That's not what I want to do." To this day, I find myself not so much in a time-warp, but very resistant to change out of my comfort zone.

You can see how important it is to teach problem-solving skills to strong-willed children. This is not just any valuable life lesson; it is an investment in their future. It prepares them for the complexities and challenges they will inevitably face in adulthood, giving them the confidence and competence to navigate life's twists and turns effectively. It empowers them to become independent, resilient, and responsible individuals who can positively affect both their own lives and society.

Teaching problem-solving skills also strengthens decision-making abilities because the two concepts are closely intertwined. As children practice identifying the problem, then gathering relevant data and information, they use analytical thinking to fully understand the context and factors involved in a decision. This is crucial for making informed choices or generating alternative solutions. Within this process, they must evaluate the consequences (the pros and cons) for each solution before they settle on a final decision. This includes assessing potential risks and benefits of different solutions. Over time they become more adept at making thoughtful choices across different aspects of their lives.

Problem-solving skills provide a firm foundation for effective decision making. The analytical, critical thinking, and problem-solving processes are highly transferable to the decision-making process. Individuals who possess strong problem-solving skills are better equipped to navigate complex decisions, assess risks, and make choices that align with their goals and objectives. These skills contribute to better decision outcomes and a more efficient and effective decision-making process.

Problem-solving skills and emotional intelligence also have an interconnected and mutually beneficial relationship. Developing problem-solving skills can enhance emotional intelligence, and having high emotional intelligence can improve one's problem-solving abilities. By understanding that problems are a natural part of life and can be addressed constructively, individuals can manage stress, anxiety, and frustration. This skill is particularly valuable for strong-willed children who might be prone to intense emotional reactions.

Managing emotions involves self-awareness, which is a fundamental component of emotional intelligence, self-regulation especially in high-pressure situations, empathy (understanding the emotions and needs of others), social skills, conflict resolution, adaptability, motivation, resilience, communication, and decision making. Problem-solving skills and emotional intelligence go hand in hand.

Developing problem-solving skills can contribute to emotional intelligence by enhancing these emotional and social competencies. Conversely, having a high level of emotional intelligence can improve one's ability to approach problem-solving with empathy, self-awareness, and effective communication, leading to more successful and emotionally intelligent solutions to challenges and conflicts. This is something that is sorely needed in the world!

And last, Problem-solving skills can teach kids how to work effectively with others through collaboration. Learning to collaborate is a valuable aspect of problem-solving, as many challenges and complex issues in life often require input, perspectives, and efforts from multiple individuals. In situations where their strong-willed nature might lead to conflicts, teaching them how to work with others to find solutions fosters teamwork, communication, and empathy.

Problem-solving usually begins with a clear definition of a shared goal. Kids learn that working together with others is essential to achieve common objectives. This includes brainstorming, pooling resources, listening to one another to hear different perspectives and approaches, which can lead to conflict resolution, task delegation and responsibility and accountability. All these collaboration skills build peer learning, respect for others, trust in their teammates, diversity of thought, and interdependence.

And to top it all off, successfully solving problems through collaboration provides a sense of achievement and reinforces the idea that working together can lead to positive outcomes. Then the kids get to celebrate their shared success, locking in the lessons learned from their teamwork.

In conclusion, teaching problem-solving skills to strong-willed children goes beyond addressing immediate challenges; it equips them with lifelong tools for success. These skills empower them to be resourceful, adaptable, creative, and confident individuals who approach difficulties with a constructive mindset. By nurturing their problem-solving abilities, you're preparing them for a future where they can navigate complexities with resilience and ingenuity.

Here are some examples of how to teach problem-solving skills to your strong-willed child:

Identifying the Problem: Engage your child in discussions about challenges they face. Ask questions like,

> How was your day today? Is there anything specific that made it great or challenging?
>
> Can you tell me about something that has been on your mind lately?
>
> Is there something you're currently struggling with or finding difficult?

Can you describe a situation at school or with friends that has been bothering you?

What do you think is the most challenging part of your schoolwork or any projects you're working on?

Is there anything you're worried about or feeling stressed about right now?

Can you share a recent experience that made you feel proud or happy?

How do you feel when you face a challenge?

What strategies or solutions have you tried to overcome a recent challenge?

Do you think talking about the challenge with someone, like a friend or a family member, would help?

What are some things that you think could make dealing with challenges easier for you?

How can I best support you when you're facing a difficult situation or challenge?

What are some goals or aspirations you have, and what challenges do you anticipate on the way to achieving them?

Can you think of a time when you faced a challenge and successfully worked through it? What did you learn from that experience?

Is there something you'd like to learn or develop that you think would help you handle challenges better?

Who are some people you admire, and how do you think they handle challenges in their lives?

If you could change one thing about how you handle challenges, what would it be?

How can we work together to tackle any challenges you're currently facing?

Are there any challenges you'd like to learn more about or explore further?

What are some strategies or techniques you've seen others use to overcome similar challenges?

These types of questions are more engaging than simply asking, "What's bothering you?" or "What's a problem you'd like to solve?" The deeper the question, the more it encourages a thoughtful answer, enabling you to recognize the issues your child may be having. Remember to create a safe and nonjudgmental space for your child to express themselves. Listen attentively, offer encouragement and support, and be patient. Building open lines of communication can help your child feel more comfortable sharing their challenges and seeking guidance when needed.

Brainstorming Solutions: Encourage your child to brainstorm potential solutions to the particular challenge or problem your child is having. Sit down together and list different ideas, even if some seem unconventional. For instance, if they're struggling with organizing their toys, suggest ideas like sorting by color, size, or type.

Weighing Pros and Cons: Teach them how to evaluate the pros and cons of each solution. Discuss the potential outcomes of different options. If they're deciding how to spend their free time, help them consider the advantages and disadvantages of each choice.

Considering Consequences: Guide them to think about the potential consequences of their choices. If they're deciding whether to finish their homework before playing, discuss how each choice might affect their evening and the next day.

Choosing the Best Solution: Help them select the most suitable solution based on the pros, cons, and consequences they've considered. For example, if they're deciding how to manage their time during the weekend, guide them in choosing activities that align with their priorities.

Implementing and Evaluating: Encourage them to put their chosen solution into action. Afterward, discuss how it worked out. If they decided to organize their study materials differently, ask if it made studying easier or if there are further improvements to be made.

Reflecting on Failures: Teach them that failures are opportunities to learn. If a solution doesn't work out as expected, help them reflect on what they've learned and how they can adjust their approach next time.

Role Modeling: Demonstrate problem-solving in your own life. When you face a challenge, discuss your thought process and the steps you take to find a solution. This provides them with a real-life example of problem-solving in action.

Encouraging Creativity: Present open-ended challenges that require creative solutions. For example, give them a scenario like "If you were stranded on a desert island, how would you find food and water?" This encourages them to think creatively and explore unconventional approaches.

Collaborative Problem-Solving: Encourage them to solve problems with others. If they're having a disagreement with a friend, guide them to discuss the issue and find a compromise together.

By teaching problem-solving skills through these methods, you empower your strong-willed child to approach challenges methodically, creatively, and confidently. These skills not only enhance their ability to handle immediate difficulties, but also contribute to their overall personal growth and development. Remember to foster a supportive and non-judgmental environment to encourage your child to explore their ideas freely, even if they seem unconventional, as all this can lead to creative breakthroughs and innovative thinking.

CHAPTER 11

AVOID POWER STRUGGLES

Avoiding power struggles with your children is crucial for fostering healthy relationships, promoting their autonomy, and creating a positive home environment. Strong-willed children, in particular, are more inclined to engage in power struggles because of their desire for independence and assertion. Recognizing and sidestepping these conflicts has many benefits for both their emotional well-being and your parenting effectiveness.

Engaging in power struggles within the parent-child relationship can have profound and detrimental effects on the bond between parents and their children. These clashes often arise when both parties seek to assert control or dominance, leading to arguments and conflicts that breed frustration and resentment. As parents and children lock horns in these battles of will, they inadvertently sow the seeds of discord that can corrode the foundation of trust and emotional connection that form the heart of a healthy parent-child relationship.

Arguments and conflicts centered on control are particularly damaging because they divert the focus from the nurturing, supportive, and understanding aspects of the parent-child dynamic. Instead of cultivating an environment where children feel safe, loved, and valued, power struggles create an atmosphere rife with tension and insecurity. Over time, this tension can erode trust, leaving children feeling misunderstood and unsupported by their parents.

To preserve and strengthen the parent-child bond, it's crucial for parents to adopt a more empathetic and collaborative approach that promotes communication, compromise, and mutual respect, rather than resorting to power struggles that only undermine the connection they share with their children.. By avoiding these struggles, you create a foundation of open communication, where your child feels safe expressing their thoughts and concerns without fear of confrontation.

Avoiding power struggles in your interactions with children is not only a way to preserve the parent-child relationship, but also a means of respecting their individuality. Strong-willed children, in particular, possess a natural drive for autonomy and a desire to assert their independence. When parents acknowledge and support this need, they provide a foundation for healthy self-esteem and self-confidence. Allowing children the space to make choices, voice their opinions, and exercise some degree of control over their lives empowers them to develop a strong sense of self. By avoiding unnecessary resistance and confrontation, parents create an environment that fosters their child's autonomy, reinforcing the idea that their thoughts and preferences matter.

When parents steer clear of power struggles and offer their children opportunities for decision-making, they not only promote autonomy but also nurture open lines of communication. This approach encourages children to express themselves, share their thoughts and feelings, and engage in meaningful dialogue with their parents. Such positive interactions strengthen the parent-child bond and help children develop vital life skills, such as problem-solving and decision-making. By respecting a child's individuality and granting them the freedom to make choices, parents not only show trust in their abilities but also foster a healthy sense of self-worth and independence that will serve them well throughout their lives.

Sidestepping power struggles within the parent-child relationship serves as a valuable opportunity to teach children the crucial skill of conflict resolution. By choosing to engage in respectful communication and problem-solving, parents become powerful role models for their children, demonstrating that conflicts need not escalate into confrontations. Instead, they can be addressed in a constructive and healthy manner. These demonstrations not only equip children with practical conflict-resolution skills but also impart the emotional intelligence necessary to navigate challenging interpersonal situations throughout their lives.

When parents model respectful communication and problem-solving, they convey several essential lessons to their children. First and foremost, they teach the significance of active listening, empathy, and understanding in resolving disputes. Second, parents demonstrate that conflicts are a natural part of relationships and can be approached with patience and respect. By offering this blueprint for constructive conflict resolution, parents empower their children to handle disagreements, negotiate solutions, and maintain positive relationships, ultimately contributing to their personal growth and emotional well-being.

Avoiding power struggles within the parent-child relationship serves as a powerful means to reduce emotional stress, not only for the child but also for the parent. Arguments and confrontations often lead to heightened emotions, with both parties becoming entangled in a cycle of frustration, anger, and stress. These emotional battles can take a significant toll on the child's mental well-being, leading to anxiety, fear, and a diminished sense of self-worth. Parents can also experience immense stress when caught up in these conflicts, as they grapple with feelings of guilt or inadequacy, struggling to navigate the fine line between discipline and authoritarianism.

Choosing non-confrontational approaches in parenting creates a calmer and more harmonious atmosphere in the household, allowing disagreements to be handled constructively. In such an environment, parents can encourage open communication, active listening, and empathetic understanding. This promotes a sense of safety and trust between parent and child, fostering healthier emotional development for the child.

By sidestepping power struggles, parents can teach their children valuable stress management skills, including how to express themselves effectively, seek compromise, and find solutions to problems without resorting to aggression or emotional turmoil. Ultimately, reducing emotional stress through non-confrontational parenting not only benefits the immediate well-being of both child and parent but also contributes to the long-term development of emotional intelligence and resilience in the child.

Avoiding power struggles in your parenting approach reinforces your authority in a more effective and sustainable manner. While it may seem counterintuitive to some, the key to establishing authority lies in setting clear boundaries and expectations while maintaining a calm and respectful demeanor. By consistently upholding these standards and addressing issues with empathy and understanding, you send a powerful message to your child: authority is not about asserting dominance or control but about nurturing a healthy and supportive environment where rules and guidance are rooted in mutual respect.

In this context, your child learns that you are a reliable and trustworthy source of guidance and support. They understand that your authority is not arbitrary but based on rational decision-making and fairness. By avoiding power struggles, you demonstrate that you are a role model for respectful behavior and conflict resolution, qualities that command genuine respect. This approach fosters a stronger parent-child bond built on trust, communication, and cooperation, which ultimately allows you to maintain your authority without resorting to confrontations or dominance-based tactics.

Avoiding power struggles with strong-willed children can be a powerful tool for nurturing their self-esteem. These children often resist authority as a way to assert their capabilities and independence. Rather than engaging in confrontations that may undermine their confidence, parents can take a more positive and empowering approach. By focusing on their strengths and providing them with opportunities to excel and show their abilities, parents can boost their child's self-esteem and discourage defiant behavior.

When parents emphasize their child's strengths and encourage them to take on responsibilities and challenges, they send a clear message that they believe in their child's abilities. This affirmation helps the child develop a healthy self-image and a sense of self-worth. It also shows them that their parents recognize and appreciate their unique qualities, fostering a positive self-identity. In this supportive environment, strong-willed children are more likely to channel their assertiveness and independence in constructive ways, ultimately benefiting from the development of their self-esteem and self-confidence.

Remember, avoiding power struggles with your children, especially strong-willed ones, is essential for building a harmonious home environment. By promoting open communication, respecting their autonomy, teaching conflict resolution, reducing emotional stress, maintaining your authority, and boosting their self-esteem, you create a positive atmosphere that encourages growth, cooperation, and mutual respect.

Here are examples of how to avoid power struggles with children, including strong-willed ones:

Offer Choices: Instead of issuing commands, offer choices within limits. For instance, instead of saying, "Put on your jacket now," you could say, "Do you want to wear your blue jacket or your red one?" "Should we go to the park or play in the backyard?"

Use Redirection: When you sense a power struggle brewing, redirect their attention to a different activity or topic. For instance, if they refuse to eat their vegetables, you could say, "Let's talk about your day at school while you take a few bites." "I understand you may not want to talk about chores right now. How about we discuss your favorite books or movies instead?" "I have a challenge for you tonight. Let's see how quickly you can brush your teeth and change into your pajamas. I'll time you, and if you beat the timer, you can pick a bedtime story." "Let's take a break from homework for a few minutes and play a quick game together. We can come back to your homework with a fresh mind."

Give Advance Notices: Provide advance notices for transitions or changes. In each of the following examples, providing advance notice allows the child to mentally prepare for the upcoming change, reducing resistance and potential tantrums. It also gives them a sense of control and a chance to finish up what they're doing, making the transition smoother and less abrupt. If it's time to leave the park, say, "We're leaving in five minutes. What's the last thing you want to do?" "In 15 minutes, it will be time to start our bedtime routine. That means it's time to finish up your game, pick out a book, and get your pajamas ready." "We have about 10 more minutes to play at your friend's house, and then it will be time to go home. What would you like to do with your friend before we leave?" "You have 5 more minutes on your tablet, and then we'll need to turn it off for today. Is there anything you'd like to finish up or save for next time?"

Use Humor and Playfulness: Diffuse tension with humor. Using humor not only diffuses tension, but also creates a more positive and enjoyable atmosphere for children. It can make tasks and transitions feel less daunting and more fun, ultimately fostering a closer and more cooperative parent-child relationship. For example, if they resist taking a bath, you could say, "Looks like the bathtub monster is hungry! Let's feed it with bubbles!"

> "Oh no, it seems like bedtime is approaching! But first, let's see if you can beat me in a 'silly walk' race to the bedroom. Ready, set, go!"
>
> "Looks like these toys are having a dance party on the floor. Let's help them find their way back to the toy box so they can rest. And maybe they'll teach us a new dance move or two!"
>
> "I heard broccoli has secret superpowers. It makes you strong like a superhero! Let's see who can eat the most and become 'Captain Broccoli' today."
>
> "Time for homework, my little genius! How about we start with the trickiest math problem ever invented, and then we'll work our way to the easy ones?"

Set Clear Expectations: Before entering a situation, discuss what's expected. By discussing and setting clear expectations in advance, you provide children with a framework for understanding their roles and responsibilities in different situations. This helps them feel more confident and prepared, reducing the likelihood of misunderstandings or conflicts. For example, before going to a store, explain that you'll only buy one treat, so they're aware of the limits. Here are some more ideas:

> "Before your friend comes over, let's talk about what's expected. We should share our toys, use our indoor voices, and be kind to our

guests. What are some other good behaviors to remember during the playdate?"

"Before we go to the park, let's discuss our expectations. We'll have fun, but we also need to stay safe. That means holding hands when crossing the street and listening when we say it's time to leave. What else do you think we should remember?"

"Before we start dinner, let's set our expectations. We'll all try a bit of everything on our plates, use polite table manners, and have a pleasant conversation. What else should we remember about mealtimes?"

"Before you begin your school project, let's talk about what's expected. We'll need to gather materials, work on it a little each day, and ask for help if we get stuck. What else do you think we should include in our plan?"

Remember to acknowledge their feelings and empathize before offering solutions. Reflecting their feelings and empathizing before offering solutions helps children to feel heard and understood. It allows them to process their emotions and encourages open communication, making it easier to work together to find solutions or cope with challenging situations. If they're upset about bedtime, you could say, "I understand you'd like to stay up, but our bodies need sleep to feel good."

"I can see you're feeling really frustrated because you can't find your favorite toy. That can be really tough. Let's work together to look for it."

"I understand you're feeling disappointed that we had to cancel our picnic because of the rain. I was looking forward to it too. How about we find a fun indoor activity to do together instead?"

"I see that you're scared of the thunderstorm outside. Thunder can be loud and scary. Would you like to cuddle with me and listen to a calming story until it passes?"

"It looks like you're really angry that your tower of blocks fell over. I can understand why you'd feel that way. Let's rebuild it together, and I'll help make it even taller this time."

Time Management: By incorporating time management strategies into their daily routines, parents can teach children valuable skills for managing their time effectively, setting goals, and becoming more organized and responsible. These skills not only benefit children in their current activities, but also prepare them for future academic and personal success.

There are many ways parents can start teaching their toddlers time management. For example, set a timer to show transitions. If it's time to stop playing and start getting ready for bed, say, "When the timer goes off in 10 minutes, it's bedtime."

My daughter-in-law had issues with her toddler waking them up at 5am. She researched until she found a solution. She found a toddler sleep training clock with a red light-green light timer. If he woke up and the light was red, he could stay in his bed or get up and play in his room if he wanted to, but he couldn't go wake mom and dad until the light turned green. It worked like magic. This simple maneuver gave his mind many things to process, such as timing, consideration for others, constructive ways of filling his own idle time, and eventually getting his body used to sleeping a little later in the morning.

Parents can create a visual schedule using pictures or words to outline the day's activities and routines. This helps children understand what to expect and start managing their time effectively. For example, a morning routine chart can include brushing teeth, getting dressed, and having breakfast, while an after-school schedule might include homework time, playtime, and dinner.

Parents can establish time limits for various activities, such as screen time, playtime, or chores. Using timers or alarms, children can learn to manage their tasks within the allotted time. For instance, setting a 30-minute timer for screen time encourages children to be mindful of their usage and transition to other activities when the timer goes off.

Parents can teach children how to prioritize tasks and assignments by encouraging them to make a to-do list or use a planner. These strategies help them organize their responsibilities. Parents can also help children identify which tasks are most important or urgent and tackle those first.

Time Blocking and Planning: Parents can introduce time blocking and planning techniques to help children manage their activities and commitments. This involves allocating specific time blocks for various tasks, such as homework, extracurricular activities, and free time. Parents can guide children in creating a weekly schedule that balances their obligations and interests.

Involving kids in finding solutions to problems and challenges can empower them to think critically and take ownership of their actions. For example, if they're reluctant to do homework, ask, "How can we make homework time more enjoyable?" By using statements and questions like this, parents can engage children in the problem-solving process, promote their critical thinking skills, and empower them to become more proactive and confident in addressing challenges they encounter in their lives. Here are some statements and questions parents can use to engage children in the problem-solving process:

"What do you think is the best way to handle this situation?" This encourages children to brainstorm their own solutions and take an active role in problem-solving.

"Can you tell me more about what's bothering you?" This opens the door for children to express their feelings and concerns, helping parents better understand the issue.

"How would you like things to be different?" This helps children articulate their desired outcomes and goals for resolving the problem.

"What ideas do you have for making this situation better?" This encourages children to come up with creative solutions and alternatives.

"What can we do together to solve this problem?" This emphasizes teamwork and collaboration between parents and children in finding solutions.

"Are there any similar situations you've encountered before, and how did you handle them?" This encourages children to draw from their experiences and problem-solving skills.

"What are the pros and cons of each solution you've thought of?" This promotes critical thinking by asking children to weigh the advantages and disadvantages of different options.

"Is there someone you trust or admire who has faced a similar challenge? What might they do in this situation?" This encourages children to seek inspiration from role models and consider alternative perspectives.

"What resources or support do you think you might need to implement your solution?" This helps children identify the tools, knowledge, or help required to put their ideas into action.

"Let's try one of your ideas and see how it works. If it doesn't, we can always come up with another plan. How does that sound?" This encourages children to take initiative and provides a sense of reassurance that mistakes are part of the learning process.

"How can we make a plan to solve this problem step by step?" This guides children in breaking down the problem into manageable tasks and developing an action plan.

"What are some potential challenges or obstacles we might encounter while implementing your solution, and how can we overcome them?" This encourages children to anticipate and plan for potential roadblocks, fostering problem-solving resilience.

Offer a Compromise: Find middle ground to avoid direct confrontations. Good statements encourage open communication, cooperation, and the search for solutions that consider both the child's and the parent's needs and preferences. They promote a more collaborative and less confrontational approach to resolving conflicts and making decisions within the family. For example, if they resist turning off the TV, suggest: "How about we finish this episode, and then it's bedtime?" This offers a good example of the parent's willingness to compromise instead of sticking to rigid bedtime rules, leading the child to do the same. Here are a few more examples.

"I understand you'd like to [child's request], and I'd like [parent's preference]. How about we meet halfway and [compromise or middle-ground solution]?"

"Let's find a solution that works for both of us. What if we [suggest a compromise or middle-ground idea]?"

"I hear what you're saying, and I have my own thoughts on this. How about we come up with a plan that includes elements of both our ideas?"

"It's important to me that you're happy, and it's also important that we [state the parent's perspective]. How can we balance both our needs?"

"I see where you're coming from, and I'd like to find a solution that makes us both happy. Can we brainstorm some options together?"

"We might have different ideas, but I believe we can find a solution that respects both of our viewpoints. What do you think about [compromise or middle-ground suggestion]?"

"I value your opinion, and I hope you can also consider my point of view. Can we work together to find a solution that takes both into account?"

"Let's try to find common ground here. How about we agree to [compromise or middle-ground proposal] as a way to address both our concerns?"

"I know we don't always agree, but I believe we can find a solution that feels fair to both of us. What if we [suggest a compromise or middle-ground approach]?"

"I want us to work together to solve this issue in a way that we both feel good about. Can we think of a compromise that respects both of our wishes?"

Positive reinforcement: This is an effective way for parents to encourage and reinforce desired behaviors in their children. Positive reinforcement statements should be specific, genuine, and focused on the behavior or trait you want to encourage. They help children understand what they're doing right and motivate them to continue displaying the desired behaviors. For example, if they clean up their toys without a struggle, say, "I noticed how responsible you are for cleaning up. Great job!" Here are some more examples:

"I'm so proud of you for [specific behavior]." This statement acknowledges and praises the child for their specific positive action.

"You did a great job with [specific behavior]. Keep it up!" This encourages the child to continue displaying the desired behavior.

"I noticed how you [specific behavior], and that's really helpful." This highlights the helpfulness of the behavior and reinforces its value.

"You're showing a lot of responsibility by [specific behavior]." This recognizes and commends the child for taking on responsibilities.

"I appreciate it when you [specific behavior]. It makes things run smoothly." This expresses gratitude for the behavior and emphasizes its positive impact.

"You're being such a good friend by [specific behavior]." This reinforces the child's positive social interactions and empathy.

"Wow, you really focused and worked hard on [specific behavior]." This recognizes the child's effort and commitment to the behavior.

"I can see that you're becoming more [specific positive trait] with your [specific behavior]." This links the behavior to the development of positive character traits.

"You remembered to [specific behavior] without being reminded. That's responsible!" This commends the child's self-starting responsible behavior.

"I knew you could do it, and you did! You [specific behavior] like a champ." This provides encouragement and reinforces the child's capability.

"You're doing such a great job with [specific behavior], and I'm really impressed." This expresses admiration and reinforces the child's efforts.

"I see how you [specific behavior], and it's making our family/team/situation better." This emphasizes the positive impact of the behavior on the family or group.

By employing these strategies, you can redirect your child's strong-willed nature toward cooperation and positive behavior, thus avoiding unnecessary power struggles and maintaining a more harmonious parent-child relationship.

CHAPTER 12

TEACH EMOTION REGULATION

Empowering a strong-willed child to grasp and effectively manage their emotions is an absolutely crucial facet of their holistic development and overall well-being. These children tend to possess exceptionally intense emotions, making it even more imperative to provide them with the tools to navigate and regulate these feelings. By doing so, parents and caregivers are not only assisting in the immediate resolution of behavioral challenges but also laying the firm foundation upon which the child can build a lifetime of healthy emotional intelligence, robust interpersonal skills, and resilient mental health. This emotional coaching is an investment in their future, equipping them with the essential life skills to thrive and excel in the complex tapestry of human interactions and emotional landscapes that await them.

First, understanding emotions empowers children to communicate effectively. When they can identify and label their feelings, they can express themselves more clearly to others. This reduces frustration and misunderstandings, fostering better relationships with peers, family members, and eventually, colleagues and friends.

Nurturing emotional awareness within your child is an indispensable step toward fostering self-control, a cornerstone of their personal growth. Guiding your child to not only identify but also comprehend their emotions when they experience anger, frustration, or distress empowers them to respond thoughtfully rather than impulsively. This critical skill is the linchpin for managing potent emotions and making well-considered decisions. It provides them with a shield against impulsive reactions, granting the ability to navigate life's challenges with a poised and deliberate demeanor, which is paramount for their success in both immediate daily situations and the lifelong journey of self-mastery.

Guiding strong-willed children in managing their emotions is a profound lesson in resilience, one that equips them to weather life's storms with unwavering strength. These children often confront challenges with an intensity that can be both admirable and daunting. However, by teaching them constructive coping strategies, parents and caregivers empower them to bounce back from setbacks and face adversity with remarkable grace. This journey toward emotional mastery instills within them not only the fortitude to confront challenges head-on but also the invaluable capacity to transform adversity into an opportunity for growth. It is a profound investment in their future, gifting them the resilience to confront life's uncertainties and emerge from them stronger and more resilient than ever before.

The cultivation of emotional intelligence exerts a profoundly positive influence on a child's mental health, a vital aspect when dealing with strong-willed individuals who often grapple with heightened intensity. These children, because of their inherent nature, may be more susceptible to stress and anxiety. However, providing them with comprehensive tools and strategies to understand and control their emotions serves as a powerful defense against the dangers of mental health challenges.

By offering these essential coping mechanisms, parents and caregivers not only help mitigate potential emotional turmoil but also actively contribute to the creation of a robust emotional well-being that empowers these children to navigate the complexities of life with resilience, grace, and a profound sense of self-assuredness.

In conclusion, the commitment to nurturing emotional intelligence in your strong-willed child goes above and beyond the role of a parent or caregiver; it becomes an enduring investment in their present and future well-being. Beyond merely facilitating the navigation of emotional maelstroms, this investment gives them an invaluable toolkit, one that empowers them to communicate with eloquence, confront stress with resilience, extend empathy to others, resolve conflicts harmoniously, and triumph in the multifaceted journey of life. The acquisition of these skills isn't just a foundation for success but a compass guiding them toward the shores of happiness, fostering profound relationships, and propelling relentless personal growth. It is a legacy of emotional wisdom that ensures their place as confident and capable individuals in a world that is forever enriched by their presence.

Emotion Identification: This is the process of recognizing one's own feelings. Emotion identification is a fundamental aspect of emotional intelligence, enabling individuals, including children, to communicate their feelings effectively, empathize with others, and make informed decisions based on their emotional states. It plays a crucial role in building self-awareness, fostering healthy relationships, and managing one's emotional responses in various life situations.

Here are some specific examples of questions you can ask your children to help them explore and identify their emotions in various contexts. For instance,

> After a playdate: "How did you feel when your friend shared his toys with you?"
>
> Social Situations: "How did you feel when you joined the school group activity and made a new friend?"
>
> School Experiences: "Can you tell me how you felt during the math test today? Were you excited, nervous, or something else?"
>
> Family Gatherings: "When we visited Grandma's house, how did you feel when you saw your cousins again after a long time?"
>
> Physical Activities: "After your soccer game, what emotions did you experience? Were you proud of your performance or disappointed about something?"
>
> Unexpected Events: "When it started raining during our picnic, how did you feel? Were you upset, surprised, or maybe even excited about the change?"

Labeling Emotions: By providing them with a vocabulary to express their emotions, children can move beyond simple labels like "happy" or "sad" and delve into a richer understanding of their inner world. This not only helps them communicate their feelings more precisely but also encourages introspection, self-awareness, and empathy for others. By learning to articulate emotions such as "frustrated," "excited," "anxious," or "content," children gain the tools to navigate their emotional landscapes effectively, resolve conflicts, and seek support when needed.

"It looks like you're feeling really excited about your upcoming birthday party!"

"When your friend shared their toy with you, how did that make you feel? Was it happiness?"

"I can see that you're feeling a bit frustrated because your puzzle pieces aren't fitting together."

"When we read that story about the sad puppy, what emotion do you think the puppy was feeling?"

"Sometimes, when we're nervous about trying something new, we might feel a little scared. Have you ever felt like that?"

"You seem very proud of the drawing you made. Is that the feeling you're experiencing right now?"

"How do you feel when you spend time with Grandma and Grandpa? Is it happiness or something else?"

"When we missed the ice cream truck, did you feel disappointed?"

"It's okay to feel a bit jealous when your brother gets a new toy. Jealousy is a common feeling sometimes."

"When we have to say goodbye to our friends after a playdate, we might feel a little sad. Does that sound like what you're feeling now?"

These sentences encourage children to explore and express their emotions, gradually building their emotional vocabulary and helping them become more adept at identifying and communicating their feelings.

Art and Expression: Encouraging children to engage in art and expression can be a powerful tool for nurturing their emotional intelligence. By providing them with art supplies and encouraging creative endeavors such as drawing, painting, or crafting, we offer a channel for them to externalize their emotions and thoughts in a visual and tangible way. This process not only allows children to explore their feelings, but also helps them understand and process those emotions on a deeper level. Art provides a safe and non-verbal outlet for complex emotions that may be challenging to express through words alone. As children translate their inner worlds onto paper or canvas, they gain insight into their emotional landscapes, fostering self-awareness and emotional clarity. This creative exploration is a therapeutic and constructive means of coping with difficult emotions, ultimately contributing to their overall well-being and personal growth.

To help a child externalize and understand their emotions through art, a parent can suggest various prompts or themes for their drawings or paintings. These prompts should be open-ended and encourage the child to express their feelings freely. Here are some examples:

"Draw a picture of a time when you felt really happy. What were you doing, and who was with you?"

"Create a painting that shows how you feel when you're playing with your best friend."

"Imagine you're a superhero with a special power related to your feelings. What would your superhero look like, and what power would you have?"

"Paint a picture of a place where you go to feel calm and relaxed. What colors would you use to show that feeling?"

"Draw a scene that represents a time when you were proud of something you accomplished. What did you achieve, and how did it make you feel?"

"Let's make a 'Feelings Wheel' with different sections for different emotions. Can you draw a face or scene that represents how you feel today?"

"Imagine you're inside a big bubble, and you can fill it with all your feelings. What would that bubble look like right now?"

"Draw a picture of something that makes you a little bit nervous or worried. How can you use your art to show that feeling?"

"Paint a picture of a dream you had recently. What emotions did you experience in the dream, and how can you capture them in your painting?"

"Let's create an 'Emotion Monster.' Draw or paint a monster that represents an emotion you sometimes feel. What does it look like, and how does it behave?"

These prompts encourage children to explore and express their emotions through art, allowing them to externalize and gain a deeper understanding of their feelings in a creative and engaging way. It also provides an opportunity for parents to open up discussions about emotions and support their child's emotional development.

Emotion Thermometer: The "emotion thermometer" is a simple yet effective tool that can help children navigate the complexities of their feelings. By creating a visual representation of various emotional states, from calm and happy to frustrated and angry, we offer children a way to pinpoint and communicate their emotions more effectively. Asking them to point to where they are on the thermometer encourages self-awareness and opens up an avenue for constructive conversations about their feelings. This not only helps children better understand their emotional fluctuations but also equips them with the vocabulary to express themselves more precisely. It's a valuable step towards emotional intelligence and provides a practical means for parents and caregivers to support their child's emotional development.

Visual representations of emotion thermometers can vary in design, but the key is to use a range of colors or images to depict different emotional states. Here are a few examples:

Color Gradient Thermometer: Use a vertical thermometer with a color gradient from blue at the bottom (representing calm) to green (happy), yellow (nervous), orange (frustrated), and red (angry) at the top. Children can point to the color that best matches their current emotional state.

Emoji Thermometer: Create a thermometer with a series of emojis that correspond to different emotions. For example, a smiling face for happiness, a calm face for calmness, a frowning face for sadness, a slightly angry face for frustration, and an angry face for anger.

Thermometer with Drawings: Draw simple illustrations or symbols next to each level of the thermometer. For instance, a calm sea or a serene sun for calm, a party hat for happiness, a tangled knot for nervousness, a clenched fist for frustration, and an erupting volcano for anger.

Thermometer with Words: Label each level of the thermometer with emotion words like "calm," "happy," "worried," "frustrated," and "angry." You can also include facial expressions next to each word to reinforce the emotions.

Animal-themed Thermometer: Use animal illustrations to represent different emotions. For example, a sleeping cat for calmness, a playful puppy for happiness, a hesitant turtle for nervousness, a buzzing bee for frustration, and a roaring lion for anger.

These visual representations can be tailored to the child's age and preferences, making it easier for them to identify and communicate their feelings. The chosen design should be engaging and easily understandable for the child to facilitate effective emotional expression and communication.

Mindfulness and Breathing: Introducing mindfulness and deep breathing exercises to children is a powerful tool for nurturing emotional well-being and self-regulation. By teaching them how to engage in deep, intentional breaths during moments of heightened emotions, we equip them with a valuable skill to help them find calm in the midst of emotional storms. It's crucial to practice these techniques together during moments of relaxation, allowing them to familiarize themselves with the process. In doing so, we provide children with a reliable coping mechanism they can employ when needed most. Mindfulness and deep breathing not only enable them to manage intense emotions, but also promote a lifelong practice of self-awareness, emotional resilience, and overall mental health. It's an invaluable gift that equips them to navigate life's challenges with composure and grace.

The following exercises are designed to introduce children to mindfulness and deep breathing in a fun and engaging way. Consistent practice can help them build emotional resilience and self-awareness, enabling them to better manage their emotions in various situations.

Belly Breathing

Have the child lie down or sit comfortably.

Place one hand on their chest and the other on their belly.

Instruct them to take slow, deep breaths in through the nose, feeling their belly rise like a balloon.

Exhale slowly through the mouth, feeling the belly fall.

Repeat several times, emphasizing the importance of slow and deep breaths.

Five Senses Exercise

Encourage the child to sit quietly and observe their surroundings.

Ask them to name five things they can see, four things they can touch, three things they can hear, two things they can smell, and one thing they can taste (or remember a taste they enjoy).

This exercise helps ground them in the present moment and fosters awareness of their senses.

Counting Breaths

Guide the child to sit or lie down comfortably.

Instruct them to close their eyes and take a deep breath in while silently counting to four.

Hold the breath for a count of four.

Exhale slowly for a count of four.

Repeat this cycle several times, focusing on the breath and counting.

Mindful Observation

Take a nature walk or simply sit outdoors.

Encourage the child to observe and describe everything they see, hear, smell, and feel.

This exercise helps them connect with the natural world and practice mindfulness in everyday settings.

Mindful Coloring

Provide coloring sheets and colored pencils.

As they color, guide them to pay attention to the sensations of coloring, the colors they choose, and the movements of their hand.

Encourage them to focus entirely on the coloring activity, letting go of other thoughts.

Imaginary Balloon

Ask the child to close their eyes and imagine they have a balloon in their belly.

With each deep breath in, the balloon inflates; with each exhale, it deflates.

This visualization exercise helps children regulate their breath and calm their bodies.

Parents may need to remind older children to practice deep breathing when their emotions begin to escalate. In the following situations, reminding older children to breathe can serve as a helpful coping strategy, allowing them to regain control over their emotions, reduce stress, and approach challenges with a clearer mindset. It's important for parents to provide gentle guidance and support during these moments.

Academic Stress: When an older child is feeling overwhelmed by schoolwork, upcoming exams, or a challenging project, reminding them to take deep breaths can help reduce anxiety and regain focus.

Sibling Conflicts: During arguments or conflicts with siblings, a parent can suggest deep breathing to help the child stay calm and avoid escalating the situation.

Social Pressures: If a teenager is feeling peer pressure or experiencing social anxiety, encouraging deep breathing can help them manage their emotions and make thoughtful decisions.

Sports or Competitive Activities: In moments of intense competition or sports-related stress, deep breathing can help an older child stay composed and perform at their best.

Family Tensions: During family disagreements or conflicts, suggesting deep breathing can help diffuse tension and promote constructive communication.

Public Speaking or Performances: Before giving a presentation or performing on stage, deep breathing exercises can help reduce stage fright and nervousness.

Transitioning to New Environments: When transitioning to a new school, moving to a different place, or facing significant life changes, deep breathing can help older children adapt to the new environment and manage anxiety.

Anger or Frustration: When an older child becomes angry or frustrated, taking a moment to practice deep breathing can help them cool down and prevent impulsive reactions.

Anxiety or Panic Attacks: For children prone to anxiety or panic attacks, deep breathing techniques can be a valuable tool for managing and preventing these episodes.

Overwhelm: When a child feels overwhelmed by a busy schedule or multiple commitments, a reminder to breathe deeply can provide a sense of calm and perspective.

Emotion Journals: Encouraging children to maintain an Emotion Journal is a powerful way to foster self-awareness and emotional understanding. By prompting them to record their feelings and the circumstances that led to those emotions, we provide a structured avenue for self-reflection. This practice allows children to not only identify and acknowledge their emotions but also uncover patterns and triggers that may be influencing their emotional responses. The act of journaling encourages introspection and empowers children to take ownership of their emotional experiences. Over time, it becomes a valuable tool for building emotional intelligence, enhancing communication skills, and navigating the intricate terrain of their feelings with confidence and clarity.

Here are five supportive things a parent can say when they recognize their child needs to write in their emotion journal. These statements offer understanding, support, and an invitation for the child to use their emotion journal as a tool for self-expression and self-reflection. They create a safe and non-judgmental space for the child to explore their emotions.

> "I noticed you've been feeling a bit upset today. Would you like some quiet time to write in your emotion journal and share what's been bothering you?"
>
> "It's okay to have bad feelings and writing them down can help you understand them better. Do you want to talk about what you're feeling in your journal?"
>
> "I'm here to listen whenever you're ready to talk, but sometimes it's helpful to write down your thoughts and emotions first. Would you like to give it a try?"
>
> "Remember, your Emotion Journal is a safe space where you can express yourself freely. If something's on your mind, writing it down can be a great way to make sense of it."
>
> "I've noticed a few changes in your mood lately. Writing in your Emotion Journal might help you figure out what's been on your mind. Would you like some time to do that?"

Role-Playing: Pretend to be characters in different emotional situations and discuss how each character might feel and react. Engaging in role-playing exercises with children, where we take on the roles of characters in various emotional situations, can be a remarkably effective way to nurture empathy and perspective-taking. As we step into these fictional shoes, we not only encourage children to explore a range of emotions but also provide a platform for open dialogue about how different people might feel and react in diverse circumstances.

This imaginative exercise allows children to see the world through different lenses, fostering an understanding that emotions vary from person to person. It promotes the development of empathy, a critical life skill that empowers children to connect with and support others on a deeper level. Role-playing not only enriches their emotional intelligence but also instills the values of compassion, tolerance, and open-mindedness that will serve them well in their interactions with people from all walks of life.

Here are six role-playing exercises suitable for exploring emotional situations and nurturing empathy in children:

Sharing Feelings

Each participant takes turns expressing an emotion they've experienced recently, such as happiness, sadness, anger, or excitement.

Encourage the child to articulate why they felt that way and how they expressed it.

Discuss and reflect on the different emotional experiences shared during the role-play.

Conflict Resolution

Create a scenario where two characters have a disagreement or conflict, such as sharing a toy or choosing a game to play.

Have the child take on the role of one character and you or another child as the other.

Encourage them to explore ways to resolve the conflict peacefully and express their emotions constructively.

Empathy in Action

Set up a situation where one character is facing a tough challenge or feeling sad.

The child takes on the role of a supportive friend or family member who shows empathy by offering comfort and understanding.

Discuss how their actions helped the character in distress, and how it made the character feel.

Changing Emotions:

Begin with a character experiencing one emotion (e.g., frustration).

Gradually transition the character's emotion to another (e.g., from frustration to happiness).

Encourage the child to explore how the character's thoughts, actions, and facial expressions change as their emotion shifts.

Bullying Prevention

Create a scenario involving a character who is being bullied, and another character who witnesses it.

Have the child take on the role of the bystander and explore different ways to support the victim and address the bully.

Emphasize the importance of empathy and standing up against bullying.

Problem Solving and Teamwork

Present a situation where two or more characters must work together to solve a problem, like building a bridge for a toy.

Assign roles to each participant and encourage them to collaborate, express their ideas, and manage any conflicts that arise.

Discuss how teamwork and communication influenced the outcome and the emotions of the characters involved.

These role-playing exercises provide children with opportunities to explore emotions, practice empathy, and develop problem-solving skills in a fun and interactive way. They also encourage open discussions about feelings, behaviors, and the importance of understanding others' perspectives.

Problem-Solving for Emotions: Discuss strategies to cope with specific emotions. For example, if they're feeling nervous about a new activity, brainstorm ways to manage that anxiety. These problem-solving discussions empower children to manage their emotions proactively by providing practical strategies tailored to specific situations. It also encourages them to develop a proactive and solution-focused mindset when facing emotional challenges.

Managing Test Anxiety

If the child is feeling nervous about an upcoming test, discuss strategies such as deep breathing exercises, creating a study schedule, or visualizing success to reduce anxiety and improve focus.

Handling Anger During Conflicts

If the child frequently experiences anger during conflicts, brainstorm techniques like counting to ten before reacting, using "I" statements to express feelings, or taking a short break to cool down before discussing the issue.

Dealing with Sadness After a Loss

If the child is feeling sadness after losing a pet or a loved one, explore coping strategies such as writing in a journal, creating a memory box, talking to a trusted adult, or engaging in activities they enjoy to help process their grief.

Overcoming Frustration with Schoolwork

If the child often feels frustrated when tackling difficult homework or projects, suggest problem-solving techniques like breaking tasks into smaller steps, seeking help from a teacher or tutor, or using online resources to understand the material better.

Addressing Social Anxiety

If the child experiences social anxiety, discuss strategies like practicing social skills through role-playing, setting small achievable social goals, or keeping a "success journal" to focus on positive social interactions.

Model emotional management in your own life. By openly sharing your own emotional experiences and showing how to regulate them in various situations, you provide valuable lessons on emotional intelligence and self-regulation that your children can observe and learn from in their own lives. For example, when you're frustrated, say, "I'm feeling frustrated, so I'm going to take a few deep breaths to calm down." Here are some more examples:

Handling Disappointment

When you face disappointment, such as plans changing unexpectedly, express your feelings by saying, "I'm feeling disappointed right now, but it's okay. I'll find a way to adapt and make the best of the situation."

Managing Stress at Work

If you experience work-related stress, demonstrate healthy coping mechanisms by saying, "I've had a challenging day, so I'm going to take a short walk to clear my mind and reduce stress."

Dealing with a Mistake

When you make a mistake, acknowledge it by saying, "I've made an error, and it's natural to feel frustrated, but I'll work on fixing it and learning from this experience."

Handling Conflict

When you encounter a disagreement or conflict with someone, model conflict resolution by saying, "I understand we have different opinions, so let's try to have a calm discussion to find a solution that works for both of us."

Expressing Gratitude

Demonstrate the importance of gratitude by saying, "I feel really grateful for the support of our family and friends. Let's take a moment to express our thanks for the positive things in our lives."

Creating a "calm down" corner for your child is a wonderful way to provide them with a designated space to manage their emotions and find comfort when needed. Remember that the goal of a "calm down" corner is to provide a supportive and nurturing space where your child can learn to regulate their emotions and find comfort during challenging moments. It should be a place they associate with positive feelings and relaxation. Designate a spot in the house where they can go to when feeling overwhelmed. Fill it with calming tools like a stress ball or soft toys. Here are a few ways to create an effective "calm down" corner:

Choose a Quiet Space: Select a quiet and relatively clutter-free area in your home where your child can have some privacy and minimal distractions.

Comfortable Seating: Place a comfortable chair, beanbag, or floor cushion in the corner where your child can sit or recline comfortably.

Soft Textures: Add soft textures such as plush pillows, cozy blankets, or a soft rug to create a soothing and inviting atmosphere.

Calming Colors: Use calming colors for the decor, such as soft blues, greens, or pastels, which can help create a serene environment.

Fidget Toys and Sensory Items: Provide fidget toys, stress balls, or sensory items like a jar with glitter or sand to engage their senses and promote relaxation.

Books or Calming Activities: Include a small selection of books, coloring materials, or calming activities like puzzles to help your child unwind.

Calming Music or Sounds: Consider playing soft, calming music or nature sounds in the corner to enhance the soothing ambiance.

Breathing Exercises: Place a poster or visual guide with deep breathing exercises on the wall to remind your child of relaxation techniques.

Personalization: Allow your child to personalize the space with a few of their favorite items, like stuffed animals or calming artwork they've created.

Visual Prompts: Display visual reminders of positive affirmations, calming strategies, or a feelings chart to help your child identify and manage their emotions.

Communication: Encourage your child to use the corner as a place to reflect, express their feelings, or simply take a break when they're upset.

Clear Boundaries: Establish clear rules that the "calm down" corner is a safe space where they can go voluntarily to calm down, and it's not a form of punishment.

Positive Self-Talk: Teach them to replace negative self-talk with positive affirmations. If they're feeling unsure about a task, encourage them to say, "I can try my best," or "I have the ability to give my best effort."

Help your child recognize when they engage in negative self-talk. Ask them to identify phrases or thoughts that make them feel anxious or discouraged. Teach your child positive affirmations that are age appropriate and tailored to their needs. For instance, "I am capable," "I can do it," or "I am strong and resilient."

Share moments when you replace negative thoughts with positive affirmations in your own life and explain how it helps you feel more confident. Use visualization exercises with your child to reinforce positive self-talk. Have them close their eyes and imagine successfully completing a task while repeating their affirmations. Don't forget to use positive reinforcement by celebrating small victories and achievements and highlighting the role of positive self-talk in their success.

Above all, encourage self-compassion. Teach your child that it's okay to make mistakes and that negative self-talk doesn't define them. Encourage self-compassion by saying, "It's normal to make mistakes, but we can learn from them and keep improving."

By incorporating these strategies into your interactions with your strong-willed child, you help them build a strong foundation of emotional intelligence, giving them the tools to understand, manage, and express their emotions in healthy and constructive ways.

And last, but not least, in this chapter—TEACH YOUR CHILDREN HEALTHY WAYS TO EXPRESS THEMSELVES AND COPE WITH FRUSTRATION. By teaching these healthy ways to express themselves and cope with frustration, you empower your strong-willed child to manage their emotions constructively, communicate effectively, and navigate challenges positively.

Here are examples of how to teach your children, especially strong-willed ones, healthy ways to express themselves and cope with frustration:

Verbal Expression

Encourage them to use words to express their feelings instead of acting out. Teach them phrases like, "I feel upset because..." or "I need help with..."

Journaling:

Provide them with a journal where they can write down their thoughts and feelings. This helps them process emotions and gain insight into their triggers.

Deep Breathing

Teach deep breathing techniques to help them calm down when frustrated. Practice taking slow, deep breaths together to demonstrate the method.

Physical Activities

Encourage them to channel their frustration through physical activities like jumping on a trampoline, dancing, or going for a bike ride.

Art and Creativity

Offer art supplies for them to draw, paint, or sculpt their feelings. This non-verbal outlet allows them to express complex emotions.

Music: Music serves as a healthy outlet for children to express themselves and effectively cope with frustration by allowing them to channel their emotions and creativity into a harmonious and constructive form of self-expression

Create a "Feelings" Board

Make a visual chart with different emotion faces and encourage them to point to how they're feeling. This helps them identify and communicate their emotions.

Use "I" Statements

Teach them to use "I" statements to express themselves assertively but respectfully. For example, "I feel frustrated when…"

Positive Affirmations

Introduce positive self-talk by encouraging them to say positive affirmations like, "I can handle this" or "I'm in control of my feelings."

Count to Ten

Teach them to take a moment to count to ten before reacting when frustrated. This pause can prevent impulsive actions or words.

Sensory Tools

Offer sensory tools like stress balls, textured objects, or squishy toys that they can manipulate to help release frustration.

Mindful Activities

Practice mindfulness exercises, such as focusing on their breath or paying attention to their surroundings. This helps them stay present and manage their reactions.

Problem-Solving

Guide them to problem-solve when they encounter frustrating situations. Encourage them to think of different solutions to the problem.

Modeling Healthy Expression

Model healthy expression of frustration yourself. Share how you handle frustration and the strategies you use to cope with it.

CHAPTER 13

TIME-OUTS

Time-outs can serve as a valuable tool in child discipline and development when used appropriately and thoughtfully. They offer a structured opportunity for children to calm down, reflect on their behavior, and learn to manage their emotions and actions in a safe and controlled manner. Time-outs provide a pause in the heat of a challenging moment, allowing both the child and the caregiver to de-escalate from a potentially stressful situation. This brief break can prevent impulsive reactions and give children the chance to regain emotional control.

Time-outs encourage self-reflection and self-regulation. When children are temporarily separated from a situation, they can contemplate their actions and consider alternative, more appropriate responses. This process helps them develop crucial skills in understanding and managing their own behavior. Time-outs reinforce boundaries and consequences. Children learn that certain behaviors have consequences, and by taking a break from an activity or situation, they understand the link between their actions and the resulting outcomes. This understanding contributes to their overall sense of responsibility and accountability.

When implemented with care and compassion, time-outs offer caregivers an opportunity to communicate with children about their feelings and behavior. During the time-out, caregivers can talk to the child about what happened, why certain behaviors are not acceptable, and how to make better choices in the future. This constructive dialogue is key to helping children learn and grow from their experiences.

Time-outs provide a designated period for children to regain control of their emotions. Being removed from a situation that may have triggered frustration, anger, or tantrums allows them to calm down and gradually gain the emotional stability needed to address the issue more rationally. During this brief respite, children can breathe, reflect on their feelings, and explore healthier ways to cope with emotional turbulence. This practice not only aids in immediate emotional regulation but also equips children with valuable lifelong skills for managing their emotions in various situations, promoting emotional intelligence and resilience.

Time-outs offer children a valuable opportunity to engage in behavior reflection. Removed from the stimulating environment that may have contributed to their disruptive actions, children can take a moment to ponder their behavior and its consequences. This self-reflection process encourages them to consider the impact of their actions on themselves and those around them. By asking themselves questions like "What did I do?" and "Why was it not okay?" children develop a deeper understanding of cause and effect, responsibility, and empathy.

Effective time-outs involve discussions with caregivers or parents, allowing children to express their thoughts and feelings about their actions and the choices they can make differently next time. This reflective aspect of time-outs not only addresses immediate behavior concerns but also fosters personal growth and responsible decision-making in children as they navigate the complexities of their social world.

Time-outs teach children that their actions have consequences. They begin to understand that engaging in inappropriate behavior can lead to a temporary withdrawal from the enjoyable activity or setting. This encourages them to take ownership of their choices and make more constructive decisions.

Learning accountability and the concept of time-outs are crucial life skills that contribute to personal growth and effective interpersonal relationships. Accountability involves taking responsibility for one's actions, decisions, and their consequences. It encourages individuals to reflect on their behavior, acknowledge mistakes, and make amends when necessary.

Time-outs provide an opportunity to pause and self-reflect in moments of conflict or stress. They help individuals cool down, regain composure, and consider the impact of their actions on themselves and others. Together, these lessons teach us that taking ownership of our actions and taking breaks to reflect and recalibrate are essential tools for personal development and building healthier connections with others.

Developing Self-Control: By consistently implementing time-outs, children gradually develop self-control skills. They learn to pause before reacting impulsively, which is a crucial life skill for handling conflicts and making thoughtful decisions as they grow older.

By consistently implementing time-outs, individuals can develop a crucial skill: self-control. Self-control is the ability to manage one's emotions, impulses, and reactions in challenging situations. Time-outs serve as a powerful tool for cultivating self-control because they encourage individuals to step back and assess their emotions and behaviors. During a time-out, one can reflect on what triggered their response and consider alternative, more constructive ways to handle the situation.

Over time, this practice helps individuals learn to regulate their emotional reactions, make more rational choices, and respond to stressors or conflicts with greater composure. Developing self-control through the use of time-outs equips individuals with a valuable skill that enhances their decision-making, relationships, and overall emotional well-being.

Time-outs play a pivotal role in preventing the escalation of tense or challenging situations. When emotions run high, people might say or do things impulsively that they later regret. Time-outs offer a critical pause button in such moments, allowing individuals to step away briefly from the situation. During this break, individuals can cool down, gain perspective, and collect their thoughts. This pause in the action helps prevent impulsive and potentially harmful reactions, giving everyone involved a chance to reflect on their emotions and motivations.

By providing a breathing space for emotional regulation, time-outs pave the way for more constructive and rational communication, ultimately diffusing tension and preventing the situation from escalating into something more contentious or damaging.

While time-outs address immediate behavior, they also serve as an essential catalyst for developing conflict resolution skills. Parents and children can have conversations about why the time-out occurred, what could have been done differently, and how similar situations can be handled better in the future. When individuals take a step back from a heated or challenging situation, they create a valuable opportunity to reflect on the core issues at hand. They also set the stage for meaningful discussions afterward. During this break, they can gain a deeper understanding of their own emotions, needs, and triggers, as well as those of the other parties involved. This self-awareness forms the foundation for effective conflict resolution, as it allows individuals to approach the situation with empathy and a clearer perspective.

Time-outs encourage individuals to consider alternative approaches to resolving the conflict. By taking this moment to pause long enough to gather their thoughts and do a quick brainstorm, they can return to the discussion with potential solutions or compromises in mind. This proactive approach can shift the focus from blaming or arguing to problem-solving and collaboration. In essence, time-outs set the stage for conflict resolution by promoting self-reflection, emotional intelligence, and the ability to generate constructive solutions, ultimately paving the way for more peaceful and mutually beneficial resolutions to disputes.

It is therefore obvious that time-outs promote communication. Time-outs provide a breather for both parents and children, allowing them to cool down before engaging in a conversation. This ensures that discussions are more productive, respectful, and focused on finding solutions rather than assigning blame.

Time-outs serve as a valuable tool in establishing a clear boundary between acceptable and unacceptable behavior, especially in the context of parenting and discipline. When a child is subjected to a time-out consequence for misbehavior, it sends a powerful message that their actions have crossed a line. This tangible consequence highlights the distinction between what is deemed acceptable conduct and what is not.

Children learn that certain behaviors lead to temporary isolation or removal from a situation, reinforcing the idea that these actions are undesirable and unacceptable within the family or societal framework. This clarity helps shape a child's understanding of boundaries and helps them internalize the concept of right and wrong conduct.

Furthermore, time-outs create an opportunity for parents to communicate these boundaries effectively. During the time-out period, parents can calmly explain to the child why their behavior was unacceptable, providing specific examples and emphasizing the importance of respecting rules and limits. This dialogue not only reinforces the boundary but also educates the child about the reasons behind it, promoting their understanding of the consequences of their actions.

Over time, consistent use of time-outs can contribute to the development of a child's self-regulation skills, as they learn to avoid crossing these established boundaries in favor of more appropriate and socially acceptable behavior. In this way, time-outs play a pivotal role in teaching children the crucial life skill of distinguishing between acceptable and unacceptable conduct.

Creating Safe Boundaries: Time-outs serve as a powerful tool in delineating the boundaries of acceptable and unacceptable behavior. This clarity is instrumental in helping children comprehend the limits of their conduct within the family or social setting, and it contributes significantly to their overall sense of security and consistency. When a child experiences a time-out consequence for their actions, they receive a clear and immediate signal that their behavior has transgressed established norms. This tangible consequence not only enforces the boundary but also communicates the seriousness of their actions.

In understanding these boundaries, children gain a sense of predictability and stability in their environment. They learn that certain behaviors are undesirable and come with consequences, while others are encouraged and rewarded. This consistency in expectations fosters a feeling of safety and security, as children know what to expect in terms of reactions to their actions.

Consequently, they develop a better grasp of the social rules and norms that govern their interactions, which is essential for their emotional and social development. Time-outs not only correct behavior but also provide children with a framework for navigating the complex world of social relationships, ultimately promoting their overall well-being.

It's important to note that while time-outs can be effective, they need to be used in a way that is age appropriate, respectful, and sensitive to the child's emotional needs. They should not be used as a punishment, but rather as a tool for teaching and guiding children toward more positive behavior and emotional regulation.

For strong-willed children, time-outs need to be approached thoughtfully to ensure they are effective in helping the child calm down, reflect, and learn. Here are some examples of time-outs tailored for strong-willed children:

Calm Down Corner: Designate a specific corner or area in your home as a "calm down" space. When your strong-willed child becomes overwhelmed or exhibits challenging behavior, guide them to the corner and let them know they can return to the activity once they feel ready to communicate calmly.

Personal Retreat: Allow your child to retreat to their bedroom or a quiet space when they're feeling frustrated. Encourage them to take a few moments to collect their thoughts and feelings before returning to the situation.

Breathing Breaks: Teach your child deep breathing techniques. When emotions run high, suggest they take a short breathing break in a designated area. This not only helps them calm down but also equips them with a valuable self-regulation skill.

Temporary Separation: If conflicts arise between siblings or playmates, suggest a short separation where each child takes some time in a different room to cool down. Emphasize that this is a moment to gather their thoughts, not a punishment.

Structured Timeout: If a specific rule is broken, apply a structured time-out. For example, if they refuse to follow a safety rule, they can have a brief time-out in a designated chair. Use this time to discuss the rule and its importance.

Cool-Down Activities: Provide a list of approved "cool-down" activities your child can engage in when feeling overwhelmed or frustrated. These might include reading a book, drawing, or playing with sensory toys.

Agreed-upon Signals: Create a signal that both you and your child recognize as a cue for taking a break. For instance, they could raise their hand, indicating they need a moment to regroup.

Guided Reflection: After a challenging situation, invite your child to sit down with you to discuss what happened. Ask open-ended questions to encourage them to think about their actions and emotions. Use this as a time for teaching, rather than scolding.

Limit Setting Break: If a strong-willed child is pushing boundaries consistently, you can implement a brief break from an activity they enjoy. For instance, if they're not following bedtime routines, they might miss out on reading their favorite story that night.

Positive Reinforcement: Use time-outs as an opportunity to encourage self-awareness. After they've calmed down, ask them how they're feeling and what they can do differently next time to handle the situation better. Offer praise for their insights.

Remember, the key to effective time-outs with strong-willed children is to maintain a positive and supportive approach. Ensure they understand that the time-out is not a punishment, but a chance to regroup and make better choices. Use these examples as a starting point, and tailor them to your child's personality, needs, and age.

CHAPTER 14

CONSISTENT CONSEQUENCES

Having consistent consequences for your strong-willed child is paramount for their overall development, behavioral growth, and the maintenance of a positive parent-child relationship. These children often thrive when they understand clear boundaries and know the outcomes of their actions. Consistent consequences provide them with a structured framework to navigate their impulses, make informed decisions, and develop a strong sense of responsibility.

First, Consistent Consequences Establish Predictability: Predictability is a cornerstone of creating a stable and nurturing environment for children, and this principle applies especially to strong-willed youngsters. Like most children, they too benefit immensely from a clear cause-and-effect relationship when it comes to their behavior.

Consistent consequences provide a roadmap for them to understand how their actions align with particular outcomes. When they can expect that a particular behavior will cause a predictable consequence, it reduces uncertainty and anxiety, offering them a sense of control over their surroundings. This predictability can be reassuring for strong-willed children who may test boundaries more frequently, as it offers them a structured framework within which they can express their independence without feeling overwhelmed or anxious about the consequences of their actions.

The establishment of consistent consequences not only enhances predictability but also aids in building trust between parents or caregivers and the child. When children see that their actions consistently lead to the same outcomes, it fosters a sense of reliability in their relationships. They come to trust that their caregivers are fair and consistent in their responses, which reinforces the emotional bond between them. This trust and predictability contribute significantly to creating a stable emotional environment, allowing strong-willed children, as well as all children, to feel secure and supported as they navigate the complexities of growing up and learning about the world around them.

One of the fundamental life lessons that consistent consequences impart to children is the concept of cause and effect. When children consistently experience predetermined outcomes for their behavior, they gradually grasp the profound connection between their actions and the resulting consequences. This understanding is pivotal for their development, as it lays the foundation for a sense of accountability and responsibility. They come to realize that their choices and actions have direct repercussions, which is a vital life skill that extends far beyond childhood. This awareness not only empowers children to make informed decisions but also helps them appreciate the importance of thinking through their actions before acting impulsively.

The lessons in cause and effect learned through consistent consequences extend to the broader social sphere. Children recognize how their behavior can affect not only themselves but also the people around them. They learn empathy and gain an understanding of the interconnectedness of actions and reactions in human relationships. This knowledge equips them with the tools to navigate social situations more effectively, fostering better communication, cooperation, and conflict resolution skills. Ultimately, consistent consequences play a pivotal role in helping children become responsible, considerate individuals who are aware of the consequences of their choices, both for themselves and the world they inhabit.

Consistent Consequences Reinforce Learning: Repetition is a fundamental principle of learning, and it holds true when it comes to teaching children about appropriate behavior, respect, and responsibility. Consistency in applying consequences serves as a repetitive reinforcement of the lessons parents and caregivers want their children to internalize.

When children encounter predictable outcomes for their actions, they have more opportunities to grasp the cause-and-effect relationships between their behavior and the consequences that follow. This repetitive reinforcement helps solidify their understanding of what is expected of them and what behaviors are deemed appropriate in various situations.

Consistent consequences provide children with a clear framework for learning and personal growth. By repeatedly experiencing the outcomes of their actions, children can refine their decision-making processes and make more informed choices in the future. Over time, this consistent reinforcement helps them develop a strong sense of responsibility and respect for boundaries, as they internalize the lessons taught through these consequences.

As a result, they are more likely to exhibit the desired behaviors consistently, and this learning process becomes an integral part of their character development. Consistent consequences serve as a powerful educational tool, reinforcing valuable life lessons that extend well beyond childhood and into adulthood.

Consistent Consequences Promote Fairness: Fairness is a fundamental concept that children inherently seek in their interactions with others, and consistent consequences play a crucial role in fostering this perception of fairness. When rules and consequences are applied consistently within a family or social setting, children perceive that the same standards apply to everyone, regardless of age, gender, or any other factor. This perception is vital because it prevents them from feeling singled out or unfairly treated.

When children observe that their parents or caregivers respond consistently to misbehavior, they come to understand that the consequences are not arbitrary or biased, but rather a product of their own actions. This transparency in the disciplinary process cultivates a sense of equality within the family and establishes a level playing field where everyone is held accountable to the same set of expectations.

The promotion of fairness through consistent consequences goes beyond just disciplinary matters. It extends to other aspects of family life, such as decision-making, sharing, and responsibilities. Children learn that the same principles of fairness apply across various domains, reinforcing their belief in the fair treatment of all family members. This sense of fairness not only encourages cooperation and a harmonious family dynamic but also imparts valuable life lessons about justice and equality that children can carry into their interactions with peers and in broader society. Consistent consequences serve as a cornerstone for instilling a strong sense of fairness and equality in children, contributing to their overall development as responsible and considerate individuals.

Consistent Consequences also support the development of Self-Discipline. Strong-willed children, characterized by their determination and persistence, can greatly benefit from the cultivation of self-discipline. Through the consistent enforcement of consequences, parents and caregivers play a pivotal role in teaching these children how to regulate their actions and exercise self-control. When strong-willed children repeatedly experience the direct correlation between their behavior and the consequences that follow, it prompts them to think critically about their actions. This process encourages them to consider the potential outcomes of their choices, leading to more thoughtful decision-making.

Moreover, consistent consequences provide strong-willed children with the opportunity to practice self-discipline in a safe and structured environment. They learn to weigh the immediate gratification of a particular behavior against the longer-term consequences, developing the ability to delay gratification and prioritize their actions based on the desired outcomes.

This skill, essential for success in various aspects of life, including academic and professional pursuits, is nurtured through the consistency of consequences. Over time, strong-willed children can harness their self-discipline to channel their determination and assertiveness into constructive endeavors, ultimately enhancing their personal growth and achievement. In this way, consistent consequences serve as a valuable tool in equipping strong-willed children with the essential skills to navigate the complexities of the world while harnessing their innate strengths.

Furthermore, consistent consequences play a critical role in discouraging manipulation, especially in the case of strong-willed children who are known for their ability to test boundaries. When consequences are applied consistently, it leaves little room for these children to exploit loopholes or attempt to negotiate their way out of rules.

Inconsistent consequences can inadvertently teach them that there is flexibility in the rules and that they can influence outcomes through persuasion or manipulation. This can lead to a pattern of behavior where they constantly challenge boundaries and seek exceptions, making it challenging for parents and caregivers to maintain order and discipline within the household.

Consistency, on the other hand, sends a clear message that rules are non-negotiable and that there are no exceptions based on persuasion or manipulation. Strong-willed children, like all children, thrive in environments with clear, well-defined boundaries. When they realize these boundaries are steadfast and not subject to change because of their attempts at manipulation, they are more likely to internalize the rules and accept them as part of the structure of the family or social setting. Ultimately, this discourages the inclination to manipulate and paves the way for a more harmonious and respectful relationship between strong-willed children and their caregivers. Consistent consequences, therefore, act as a powerful deterrent against manipulation, helping children understand that rules are meant to be followed without exceptions.

In conclusion, having consistent consequences for your strong-willed child is a cornerstone of effective parenting. It establishes predictability, teaches cause and effect, reinforces learning, promotes fairness, cultivates self-discipline, and prevents manipulation. By providing them with clear guidelines and predictable outcomes, you empower them to navigate their world with greater understanding, responsibility, and respect for rules and boundaries.

Natural and logical consequences are effective ways to help strong-willed children understand the outcomes of their actions and learn from their choices. Here are some good examples of natural and logical consequences for rule breaking:

Natural Consequence - Forgetting a Jacket: If your child refuses to wear a jacket on a chilly day despite your advice, they might feel cold when they go outside. Experiencing the natural consequence of feeling uncomfortable because of their choice helps them understand the importance of listening to your advice.

Logical Consequence - Not Finishing Homework: If your child consistently doesn't complete their homework, a logical consequence could be having to finish it during playtime or missing out on a preferred after-school activity. This teaches responsibility and time management.

Natural Consequence - Broken Toy: If your child mishandles or throws a toy and it breaks, the natural consequence is that they no longer have that toy to play with. This helps them understand the importance of taking care of their belongings.

Logical Consequence - Unfinished Chores: If your child neglects their chore responsibilities, a logical consequence could be a reduction in screen time or privileges until they complete the chores. This teaches accountability and the importance of contributing to the household.

Natural Consequence - Not Wearing Sunscreen: If your child refuses to apply sunscreen and ends up with a sunburn, they experience the natural consequence of discomfort. This helps them learn the importance of sun protection.

Logical Consequence - Not Sharing: If your child consistently refuses to share toys with others, a logical consequence could be that they won't have the opportunity to play with those toys during group playdates. This teaches cooperation and empathy.

Natural Consequence - Messy Room: If your child's room becomes too messy, a natural consequence could be that they struggle to find things they want to play with. This encourages them to take responsibility for keeping their space organized.

Logical Consequence - Disrespectful Language: If your child uses disrespectful language towards a family member, a logical consequence might involve a brief time-out from the conversation until they're ready to communicate respectfully.

Natural Consequence - Skipping Meals: If your child refuses to eat a meal, the natural consequence is that they might feel hungry later. This helps them understand the importance of eating balanced meals.

Logical Consequence - Breaking a Screen Time Limit: If your child consistently exceeds the agreed-upon screen time, a logical consequence could be a reduction in screen time the following day. This teaches them to manage their time effectively.

Remember that the goal of natural and logical consequences is to teach and guide, not to punish. Always ensure that the consequences are reasonable, age-appropriate, and discussed with your child to help them understand the connection between their actions and the outcomes.

CHAPTER 15

QUALITY TIME

Spending quality time with your strong-willed child is a cornerstone of building a strong, trusting, and nurturing parent-child relationship. These children possess distinct personalities and often seek independence, but the time you invest in them has profound implications for their emotional well-being, behavior, and overall development.

Quality time plays a pivotal role in nurturing a deep and meaningful connection between parents and children. When you engage in activities that hold significance for both you and your child, it creates valuable opportunities for open and heartfelt conversations, shared laughter, and a strong sense of bonding. These moments of genuine connection go beyond mere physical presence; they represent the emotional investment you make in each other's lives. Through quality time spent together, you show your genuine interest in your child's thoughts, feelings, and experiences, which, in turn, encourages them to share their inner world with you.

This profound sense of connection is a cornerstone of a healthy parent-child relationship. It sends a powerful message to your child that they are not just a part of the family but a cherished and valued individual. This feeling of being understood, accepted, and loved for who they are reinforces the foundation of trust and emotional security in your relationship. It creates a safe space for your child to express themselves, seek guidance when needed, and navigate the challenges of growing up with confidence. Ultimately, quality time is not just about the activities themselves but about the precious moments of connection and affirmation that strengthen the bond between parent and child, contributing to their overall well-being and development.

Investing time together with your strong-willed child serves as a foundation for building and strengthening trust within your parent-child relationship. While strong-willed children often display a strong sense of autonomy and independence, they also greatly value knowing that you, as a parent or caregiver, are readily available to listen, support, and share moments with them. This availability is a key component in reinforcing their trust in you as a reliable and guiding figure in their life.

When you consistently spend quality time with your strong-willed child, you convey a clear message that you are not just present in their life physically but emotionally as well. Your willingness to engage in activities that interest them, to lend an ear when they want to express themselves, and to actively take part in their world shows your commitment to understanding and supporting them. This fosters a deep sense of trust because they know you are a dependable source of guidance and support, even as they navigate the complexities of asserting their independence.

Building trust through shared experiences and quality time goes beyond just fostering a sense of safety and emotional security. It also lays the groundwork for open and honest communication, where your strong-willed child feels comfortable coming to you with their concerns, questions, and challenges. This trust in your availability and understanding paves the way for a more harmonious and cooperative parent-child relationship, where you can work together to navigate the unique strengths and challenges that strong-willed children often bring to the table. Ultimately, spending time together becomes a powerful tool for nurturing trust and connection, which are essential for their emotional development and overall well-being.

Quality time provides an invaluable platform for positive reinforcement in your relationship with your child. When you engage in meaningful activities together, it offers you ample opportunities to acknowledge and praise their efforts, achievements, and good behavior.

This positive reinforcement bolsters their self-esteem and motivation significantly, encouraging consistent exhibition of positive traits.

Your child understands that their actions and choices are valued and appreciated when you openly recognize and celebrate their accomplishments. This contributes to a healthy sense of self-worth and self-confidence, fostering a positive self-image that can affect various facets of their life. When you take the time to applaud their hard work and positive behavior during your shared moments, it reinforces the idea that these actions lead to positive outcomes and that their efforts are worthwhile.

This positive feedback loop can be a powerful motivator, encouraging your child to continue making constructive choices and striving for success in different areas of their life. Ultimately, quality time becomes not just an opportunity for bonding, but a nurturing environment for the development of your child's self-esteem and a strong sense of personal motivation.

Spending quality time with your child is a remarkable window into their world, offering you a deeper understanding of who they are. Through these interactions, you have the chance to observe their interests, challenges, and strengths firsthand. By immersing yourself in their activities and conversations, you gain valuable insights into their developing personality, preferences, and developmental milestones. This firsthand knowledge is a crucial tool for tailoring your parenting approach to their unique needs and fostering a more supportive and effective parent-child relationship.

Quality time provides an ideal platform for building a stronger emotional connection. When you engage in shared activities, have open conversations, and actively take part in your child's life, you not only learn about them, but also convey your genuine interest and care. This emotional connection serves as the foundation for effective communication and empathy, allowing you to better address their concerns, fears, and aspirations. You can have a profound impact on their sense of security and trust in your relationship by being more attuned to their emotional well-being and responsive to their needs.

Spending quality time is a two-way street where you learn more about your child, and they feel valued and understood, creating a stronger and more meaningful bond between you both. Quality time also supports emotional development. Engaging in activities that encourage self-expression and conversation helps them learn to articulate their feelings, which is crucial for developing emotional intelligence and effective communication skills.

Quality time spent with your child is a powerful tool for behavior management. When you cultivate an emotional connection through shared activities and meaningful interactions, your child is more likely to respond positively to your guidance and discipline. This connection creates a sense of trust and mutual respect in your relationship, making them more receptive to your guidance and less inclined to engage in challenging behaviors. They are more likely to internalize the values and expectations you've set forth because they understand that your guidance comes from a place of care and understanding. This can lead to a reduction in difficult behavior as your child becomes more motivated to cooperate and contribute positively to your family dynamic.

Quality time serves as a foundation for effective behavior management by strengthening the emotional bond between you and your child, making your guidance and discipline more impactful and reinforcing a harmonious and respectful parent-child relationship.

Quality time with your child serves as a catalyst for their learning and exploration. By actively taking part in activities that align with their interests or by introducing them to new experiences, you ignite their curiosity and stimulate a love for learning. These shared moments of discovery not only provide valuable educational opportunities but also create a positive and nurturing environment that encourages intellectual growth.

When you show children that you appreciate their interests and are open to discovering new things together, they become more motivated to inquire, search for answers, and cultivate critical thinking abilities. Quality time becomes an educational journey filled with wonder and excitement, promoting a lifelong passion for learning and supporting your child's intellectual development.

Spending quality time together with your child plays a pivotal role in building their resilience. When you actively support them through challenges, setbacks, and even failures, you show you are a steadfast source of comfort and encouragement. This emotional support not only helps them navigate difficult situations more effectively but also instills in them the confidence to face adversity with resilience.

By being there during their tough moments and offering reassurance, you teach them valuable coping strategies and problem-solving skills. The bond formed through shared time and your unwavering support becomes the building blocks of their resilience, equipping them to bounce back from life's challenges with strength and determination.

Quality time spent with your child serves as an invaluable platform for the development of essential social skills. When you engage in shared activities, whether they involve games, projects, or conversations, you create opportunities for your child to learn cooperation, teamwork, and conflict resolution. These interactions teach them the importance of working together, considering others' perspectives, and finding common ground. Through these experiences, they gain valuable insights into the dynamics of relationships, preparing them for successful interactions with peers, teachers, and other authority figures.

Quality time fosters effective communication, as it encourages open and honest exchanges between you and your child. This practice of actively listening to one another and expressing thoughts and feelings in a safe and supportive environment nurtures their ability to articulate ideas, empathize with others, and understand nonverbal cues. These skills are not only vital for building healthy friendships, but also for navigating various social situations and establishing positive connections with people from diverse backgrounds. Quality time then becomes a training ground for the development of social competence, equipping your child with the tools they need to thrive in their interactions with others throughout their life.

I cannot overstate the immense significance of spending quality time with your strong-willed child. It transcends mere entertainment; it is an invaluable investment in their holistic development—emotionally, socially, intellectually, and behaviorally. Your active involvement communicates a profound message: *you prioritize and cherish their presence in your life.*

This investment not only nurtures their confidence, well-being, and growth, but also lays the foundation for them to grow into resilient, responsible, and empathetic individuals. In the tapestry of their life, the threads of these shared moments weave a strong, enduring bond that empowers them to thrive in a world filled with challenges and opportunities.

Here are examples of how to spend quality time with your strong-willed child:

> **Outdoor Adventures:** Go for a hike, nature walk, or bike ride together. Explore a park, forest, or trail and engage in conversations about the environment, plants, and animals you encounter.
>
> **Art and Creativity:** Set up an art station with various materials like paints, clay, or markers. Create artwork together, share ideas, and appreciate each other's creativity.
>
> **Cooking or Baking:** Choose a recipe and cook or bake a meal or treat together. This activity allows for cooperation, following instructions, and enjoying the delicious results.
>
> **Board Games or Puzzles:** Play board games or work on puzzles as a team. These activities encourage critical thinking, strategy, and friendly competition.
>
> **Reading Time:** Share a book or take turns reading to each other. Discuss the story, characters, and lessons learned from the reading material.
>
> **Science Experiments:** Conduct simple science experiments at home. Explore concepts like mixing colors, creating volcanoes, or growing crystals while explaining the science behind them.
>
> **Gardening:** Plant flowers, herbs, or vegetables together in the garden or in pots. Discuss the growth process, care needed, and the satisfaction of nurturing plants.

Build and Create: Build structures using building blocks, Legos, or other construction toys. Collaborate on a project, discuss design ideas, and celebrate your finished creation.

Music and Dance: Play musical instruments or have a dance party in the living room. Encourage them to express themselves through music and movement.

Nature Scavenger Hunt: Create a scavenger hunt list with items found in nature and go on a hunt together. This activity combines exploration, observation, and fun.

Cooking Together: Involve your child in meal preparation, from choosing ingredients to helping with cooking. Discuss healthy eating habits and the importance of balanced meals.

DIY Crafts: Work on DIY crafts such as making friendship bracelets, decorating picture frames, or creating homemade greeting cards.

Visit a Museum or Zoo: Plan a trip to a local museum, zoo, or educational center. Explore exhibits, engage in interactive displays, and learn together.

Stargazing: On a clear night, spend time stargazing. Point out constellations and discuss astronomy and the wonders of the universe.

Volunteer Together: Take part in a volunteer activity or community service project together. This fosters a sense of empathy and teaches the importance of giving back.

Remember, the essence of spending quality time with your strong-willed child lies in the magic of choosing activities that resonate with their unique interests and personalities. These shared experiences don't just result in fleeting moments; they forge indelible memories and, more importantly, serve as the crucible for learning, deepening bonds, and nurturing their unparalleled growth. In the symphony of their life, these shared moments become the crescendo, the soaring notes that harmonize the melody of their development, setting the stage for a future filled with promise and possibility.

CHAPTER 16

SEEK PROFESSIONAL HELP

Seeking professional help when behavioral issues persist or become severe in your strong-willed child is a crucial step in ensuring their well-being, development, and future success. While parenting strategies and support play a significant role, sometimes specialized intervention from professionals becomes essential for addressing underlying concerns.

Foremost, seeking professional help offers the crucial advantage of expert assessment. Behavioral issues in children can often be intricate, arising from a multitude of factors, such as emotional turbulence, developmental complexities, or underlying psychological challenges. In the capable hands of professionals like pediatricians, child psychologists, or behavioral therapists, you gain access to an extensive reservoir of knowledge and specialized tools.

The professionals embark on the meticulous journey of conducting comprehensive assessments, peeling back the layers of complexity, and skillfully uncovering the root causes of the issues at hand. This expertise not only sheds light on the intricate tapestry of your child's unique needs but also charts the course for a customized and effective intervention strategy, illuminating the path towards positive growth and transformative change.

Early intervention is key. Addressing behavioral challenges promptly can prevent them from escalating into more serious problems. Strong-willed children might be more prone to persistent behavioral issues, and seeking help early can lead to effective strategies for managing their behavior and preventing negative patterns from solidifying.

It's essential to recognize that behavioral issues in children often manifest as complex and multifaceted challenges. One of the pivotal advantages of seeking professional help is the expertise these individuals bring to the table. Pediatricians, child psychologists, and behavioral therapists possess the knowledge and experience necessary to develop highly personalized strategies tailored to your child's specific temperament, needs, and circumstances.

These tailored approaches consider the intricate interplay of factors contributing to behavioral issues, whether they stem from emotional struggles, developmental hurdles, or psychological complexities. By crafting interventions that align closely with your child's unique profile, these professionals maximize the likelihood of successful outcomes.

These strategies are not one-size-fits-all; rather, they are finely calibrated to resonate with your child's distinct challenges, offering a more precise and effective roadmap towards positive behavioral change and overall well-being. Seeking professional help affords you the benefit of an individualized and holistic approach, ensuring that your child receives the most appropriate and effective support for their specific needs.

Professional intervention offers a unique advantage in providing a neutral and impartial perspective. When dealing with behavioral issues in children, parents and caregivers sometimes find it challenging to gain a clear understanding of what's happening because they are too emotionally invested or too close to the situation. In such cases, the objective viewpoint of a trained professional, such as a pediatrician, child psychologist, or behavioral therapist, becomes invaluable. Their neutrality allows them to approach the situation without biases or preconceptions, enabling them to uncover insights that might not be readily apparent to those intimately involved.

This fresh perspective can help to peel back the layers of complexity surrounding the behavioral issues, allowing for a more comprehensive understanding of the root causes. Armed with this deeper insight, professionals can then collaborate with parents and caregivers to design interventions that are not only evidence-based but also highly targeted to address the specific underlying factors contributing to the challenges. Professional intervention acts as a vital compass, guiding the way towards a more nuanced understanding and effective resolution of behavioral issues in children, all within a supportive and objective framework.

Seeking professional help extends its benefits beyond addressing the child's behavioral issues; it significantly affects the parent-child relationship as well. When parents grapple with severe behavioral challenges without adequate support, it can create a tremendous strain on their relationship with their child. The frustration, confusion, and stress that often accompany these difficulties can inadvertently erode the sense of trust and connection between parent and child.

Seeking professional guidance serves as a vital lifeline, offering parents the tools, strategies, and insights they need to manage and address these issues effectively. This external support system not only helps ease the overwhelming burden on parents but also allows them to refocus their energy on nurturing a positive and healthy bond with their child.

By working collaboratively with professionals, parents can gain a better understanding of their child's needs and challenges. This newfound knowledge equips them with the skills to respond more effectively to their child's behaviors, creating an environment where open communication and mutual respect can thrive.

Ultimately, the parent-child relationship benefits from the relief of stress and tension, enabling both parties to rebuild trust, rebuild connection, and embark on a journey of healing and growth together. In this way, seeking professional help not only addresses the immediate behavioral issues but also fortifies and restores the fundamental bond between parent and child, paving the way for a more harmonious and nurturing relationship.

Professionals offer a lifeline for parents dealing with severe behavioral challenges in their children by providing them with invaluable coping strategies. These challenges can often be emotionally and mentally overwhelming for parents, leading to a sense of helplessness and frustration. However, professionals in fields like child psychology, pediatric medicine, and behavioral therapy not only work directly with the child, but also recognize the importance of supporting and empowering parents. They equip parents with a diverse toolkit of coping mechanisms, communication strategies, and practical tools to manage difficult situations more effectively. These resources help parents regain a sense of control and confidence in their parenting journey.

Through professional guidance, parents learn how to navigate challenging behaviors, set appropriate boundaries, and respond constructively to their child's needs. They gain insights into the underlying causes of the issues and develop a deeper understanding of their child's perspective. This knowledge not only empowers parents but also strengthens their resilience in the face of ongoing challenges. By imparting these coping strategies, professionals not only ease the immediate stress but also prepare parents for the long-term task of guiding their child towards positive behavioral changes. Ultimately, the support and guidance provided by professionals empower parents to become more effective caregivers and advocates for their child's well-being, leading to a more harmonious and nurturing family dynamic.

Seeking professional help is crucial because it allows for the identification of coexisting conditions that may underlie or exacerbate behavioral issues in children. Often, behavioral challenges are not isolated problems; they can be symptomatic of more complex issues such as Attention Deficit Hyperactivity Disorder (ADHD), anxiety disorders, or sensory processing disorders. These coexisting conditions can significantly affect a child's behavior, and without proper recognition and treatment, they may remain unaddressed, leading to ongoing challenges for both the child and their caregivers.

Professional assessment and evaluation are vital in untangling these complex cases. Pediatricians, child psychologists, and specialized therapists undergo training to recognize the signs and symptoms of coexisting conditions. Through comprehensive assessments and diagnostic tools, they can pinpoint any underlying issues that may be contributing to the behavioral challenges.

Once professionals identify these conditions, they can guide parents and caregivers towards appropriate treatment strategies, which may include therapy, medication, or specialized interventions. This not only helps ease the behavioral symptoms but also addresses the root causes, providing a more holistic and effective approach to improving the child's overall well-being. Essentially, seeking professional help ensures that professionals identify and manage any coexisting conditions appropriately, allowing the child to receive comprehensive care for optimal development and a better quality of life.

Additionally, professional assistance provides the unique benefit of a multidisciplinary approach to handling behavioral problems in kids. The challenges that strong-willed or behaviorally complex children face often extend beyond a single domain. These issues can encompass the emotional, cognitive, social, and educational aspects of a child's life. Seeking professional guidance means accessing a diverse team of experts, including child psychologists, therapists, educational specialists, and sometimes even pediatricians, who can work collaboratively to develop a holistic intervention plan. This comprehensive approach ensures that all facets of the child's development and well-being are considered.

Through this multidisciplinary collaboration, professionals pool their expertise to create a tailored strategy that addresses the child's unique needs. For example, a child struggling with behavioral issues may require not only behavioral therapy but also support in developing emotional regulation skills, improved communication, and targeted educational interventions. By working together, these professionals can craft an intervention plan that considers all these dimensions, fostering a well-rounded and effective approach. This approach not only maximizes the chances of success but also provides a more nuanced and complete understanding of the child's strengths and challenges, resulting in a more comprehensive and holistic intervention plan that supports their overall development.

Seeking professional help when behavioral issues persist or intensify in your strong-willed child is not just a proactive step but a deeply responsible one. It embodies a comprehensive approach that encompasses expert assessment, early intervention, tailored strategies, a neutral perspective, advantages to the parent-child relationship, valuable coping tools for parents, identification of potential coexisting conditions, and the strength of a multidisciplinary team. By embracing this multifaceted support system, you show a profound commitment to your child's growth, well-being, and future success. This decision not only provides immediate relief and solutions but also sets the stage for a brighter, more harmonious, and more promising future for both you and your child.

It's essential to work closely with professionals who specialize in the specific needs of your child. A multidisciplinary approach, involving collaboration among these professionals, can often yield the most effective results when addressing complex and persistent behavioral issues in children. Here are several avenues of professional help available for children with persistent or intensifying behavioral issues:

Pediatricians: Start with a visit to your child's pediatrician. They can assess your child's physical health and development, as some behavioral issues may have medical causes or be exacerbated by health-related factors.

Child Psychologists: Child psychologists specialize in understanding and addressing behavioral and emotional challenges in children. They can provide assessments, therapy, and strategies for managing these issues.

Behavioral Therapists: Behavioral therapists focus on modifying specific behaviors through evidence-based techniques such as Applied Behavior Analysis (ABA). They can help children and their families implement behavior management plans.

Child Psychiatrists: In cases where there may be underlying mental health conditions contributing to the behavioral issues, child psychiatrists can provide diagnosis and medication management, if necessary.

Speech and Language Therapists: Communication difficulties can contribute to behavioral challenges. Speech and language therapists can work with children to improve their communication skills, which can reduce frustration and problem behaviors.

Occupational Therapists: Occupational therapists can address sensory processing issues, motor skill difficulties, and self-regulation challenges, all of which can affect behavior and emotional well-being.

Educational Specialists: If the behavioral issues are affecting a child's performance at school, educational specialists, such as special education teachers or school counselors, can provide support and accommodations.

Family Therapists: Family therapists can work with the entire family to improve communication, understanding, and dynamics, which can have a significant impact on a child's behavior.

Social Workers: Social workers can help families access community resources, provide counseling, and help navigate various challenges that may be contributing to the behavioral issues.

Early Intervention Programs: For younger children, early intervention programs can provide assessments and support services to address developmental and behavioral concerns.

Support Groups: Joining support groups for parents of children with behavioral issues can provide emotional support, practical advice, and a sense of community.

School-Based Services: Many schools offer counseling services, behavior intervention plans, and Individualized Education Plans (IEPs) to address behavioral challenges within the educational setting.

Here are some resources and organizations that can help connect families with professional help for children:

American Academy of Child and Adolescent Psychiatry (AACAP): AACAP provides a "Find a Psychiatrist" tool on their website to locate child and adolescent psychiatrists in your area.

Psychology Today: Their online directory allows you to search for child psychologists, therapists, and psychiatrists by location, specialization, and insurance coverage.

National Association of School Psychologists (NASP): If you are looking for support within the school system, NASP provides resources and can help you find a school psychologist.

Autism Speaks: For families dealing with autism spectrum disorders, Autism Speaks offers a directory to help find autism specialists and resources.

National Alliance on Mental Illness (NAMI): NAMI provides information, support, and resources for families dealing with mental health challenges in children and adolescents.

Local Mental Health Authorities: Many regions have local mental health authorities or community mental health centers that offer services for children and families. A quick internet search or inquiry with your healthcare provider can help you locate these resources in your area.

Child Find: Child Find is a program under the Individuals with Disabilities Education Act (IDEA) that helps identify children with developmental delays or disabilities. Contact your local school district or education department for information on how to access their services.

Early Intervention Programs: In the United States, early intervention services for children from birth to age three can be accessed through your state's Early Intervention program. These programs provide developmental assessments and therapies.

Local Support Groups: Local support groups and parent networks can be valuable resources for connecting with other families who have experienced similar challenges and can offer recommendations for local professionals.

Children's Hospitals and Clinics: Many children's hospitals have behavioral health departments with experts in child psychology, psychiatry, and developmental pediatrics.

Family Physicians or Pediatricians: Your child's primary care provider can be a valuable resource for referrals and initial assessments.

Online Mental Health Platforms: Some online platforms, like BetterHelp and Talkspace, offer therapy services for children and adolescents, often through licensed child therapists.

Remember that the availability of these resources may vary by location, and it's essential to consult with your child's healthcare provider or pediatrician for guidance on accessing the most appropriate professional help for your child's specific needs.

It's crucial to emphasize that while internet searches and online information can provide valuable insights and guidance, they should never be seen as a replacement for the expertise and guidance of a medically trained physician or professional. Medical professionals have years of education, training, and experience that enable them to make informed assessments, diagnoses, and treatment recommendations based on a comprehensive understanding of your individual health and medical history. They can provide personalized care and ensure that your specific needs and circumstances are considered. Therefore, for any health-related concerns or decisions, it is always advisable to consult with a qualified healthcare provider or specialist who can offer professional guidance, conduct proper assessments, and provide the most appropriate medical advice and care.

HAPPY PARENTING!

ABOUT THE AUTHOR

Tosca Haag, born in Houston, Texas, is a writer and self-published author with works on Amazon. Her four successful children provided the insights for her latest book. Currently residing in San Antonio with her husband of nearly 50 years, Tosca is diligently working on her next literary project.

www.ingramcontent.com/pod-product-compliance
Lightning Source LLC
Chambersburg PA
CBHW052057110526
44591CB00013B/2245